# AFTERMATH

**An Anthology of poems in English from Africa, Asia, and the Caribbean**

**edited by Roger Weaver and Joseph Bruchac**

with introductory essays by G.S. Sharat Chandra, Osmond Enekwe and Bruce St. John

## PREFATORY NOTE

Although the Commonwealth is now disparaged, and for good reason, one of its finest legacies is the English poetry resulting from the necklace of British schools around the world. Yet most of our anthologies persist in reiterating a hierarchy and tradition which is tirelessly repetitive and limited to England proper or America. Consequently many of the fine poems in the language from other countries are not seen, particularly in America.

This anthology presents a cross-section of poets originating outside England proper and North America and who have been exposed to English-speaking schools at some point in their lives. No attempt has been made to ape an Anglo-American literary establishment or to create a new one. Poems were selected because they pleased and touched on timeless themes, or because they had something to say in relation to the major issues or our time, such as race relations, inequality, and the relations between the sexes. Whenever possible, I have selected poems which other editors have chosen, merely as a double-check on quality, but in no instance was a poem included which did not commend itself in some way. Limitations of space prevented representation from Canada where many fine poets are recognized. We are most concerned about cultural slights which may have been made inadvertently, especially to the Third World.

In order to avoid establishing another minor and arbitrary canon, the emphasis here is on poems, not poets. Hence many poets that other editors might have picked as "representative" are not included.

Roger Weaver
Corvallis, Oregon

# INTRODUCTION

The contemporary literature of other nations, aside from those of Western Europe, is very little known in the United States. This is, perhaps, understandable when we consider works of literature written in other languages. The problem of the availability of good and readable translations is a continuing one. Unfortunately, however, most North Americans are also unaware of the significant body of work written in English throughout the world, *outside of* Canada, England, Australia and the United States. In Asia, the Caribbean and Africa, a large number of talented writers use the English language as their first, and in some cases only, vehicle of expression. English is so widely used throughout the African continent, in fact, that it is a lingua franca in a considerable number of nations and has been defended as an *African* language by a number of African writers. Many well-meaning Americans do not realize just how ill-informed and patronizing they are being when they compliment a person from Ghana or Nigeria, Kenya or Zambia, on their English and then ask them where they learned to speak "our" language so well.

One of the few positive aftermaths of the colonial period — which has still not ended — has been the enrichment of world literature by an impressive and growing number of writers, from many nations, who write in English. Some of them have received the recognition they deserve. V.S. Naipul of Trinidad, descendent of immigrants from India, is regarded as one of the great novelists of the second half of the 20th Century. He and Chinua Achebe, the Nigerian writer whose works have been assigned reading in college classrooms throughout the world for the past two decades, are widely regarded as future candidates for the Nobel Prize in Literature. At present, however, most of the writers who use the English language and are not from the Western World have remained relatively obscure.

In this anthology we have gathered together what I feel to be some of the best and most exciting poetry being written in the English language today. Some of the poets are well known, Wole Soyinka of Nigeria, for example, or Edward Brathwaite of Barbados, and have reached a large number of readers outside their native lands. Some of them are new writers, appearing in print for almost the first time, such as Robert Lee of St. Lucia, Sydney Sepamla of South Africa and D. Parameswaran of India. But all of them share, in addition to their use of a common tongue, high creative ability. We are cetain that anyone who reads this collection will find more than one poet of whom they have not heard before and whom they will feel deserves to be better known.

For the sake of convenience we have divided this anthology into three sections: Africa, Asia and the Caribbean. For each section we have asked one of the poets represented to write some kind of an introduction, and in those prefatory remarks by Osmond Enekwe, Bruce St. John and G.S. Sharat Chandra the reader may find some useful directions towards a better understanding of the poems they will be reading. We have also, again for the sake of convenience, arranged each section alphabetically and according to the nation of the poet. I hope that this will not prevent anyone from seeing the many connections which also exist from poet to poet and section to section. Wole Soyinka, in a recent essay, makes an interesting point about the problems of defining the importance — or even *existence* — of African literature to an audience of *aliens* and *self-alienated Africans*. It is my belief that the writers in *Aftermath* are those who have broken the chains of self-alienation and, through their writing, have communicated with those who might once have been *aliens* but now are simply sisters and brothers from different traditions who share a common humanity. It is to that common humanity that my own small efforts in putting together this anthology are dedicated.

Peace,

Joseph Bruchac

I would like to express my gratitude to certain individuals who, through their efforts, have made *Aftermath* a much more comprehensive and meaningful book. Ezekiel Mphahlele was directly responsible for the inclusion of a number of new South African poets. Bonnie Crown of the Asian Literature Program introduced us to the Pakistani poets and the work of U Win Pe and Jyotirmoy Datta. Bruce St. John was the mainstay of our Caribbean sections, as his impressive introduction to that section suggests. Others, too numerous to mention, were of assistance at various stages of the development of this book to Roger Weaver and myself. To them I say Thank You!

**Acknowledgement Is Gratefully Extended To The Following:**

**Kofi Anyidoho** for "Our Birth-cord" and "Radio Revolution".

**Mbella Sonne Dipoko** for "Exile" and "Our Life" from *Modern Poetry from Africa*, Peguin Books, Baltimore Maryland.

**Lenrie Peters** for "Parachute Men say..." from *Satellites*, Africana Publishing Corp., NYC.

**G. Adali-Mortty** for "Village Nights" from *Messages*, Africana Publishing Corp., NYC.

**Ama Ata Aidoo** for "Cornfields in Accra" from *The New African Magazine*, Accra, Ghana.

**Jawa Apronti** for "Funeral" from *Modern Poetry From Africa*, Penguin Books, Baltimore, Maryland.

**Kofi Awoonor** for "Afro-American Beats" from *Ride Me Memory*, Greenfield Review Press, Greenfield Center, N.Y.

**Kwesi Brew** for "Dirge" and "Ancestral Faces" from *The Shadows of Laughter*, Longmans and Green, London, England.

**Joe De Graft** for "The Old Sea Chain" from *Messages*, Africana Publishing Corp., NYC.

**Kojo Gyinaye Kyei** for "African in Louisiana" and "The Talking Drums" from *The Lone Voice*, Ghana University Press, Accra, Ghana.

**Efua Sutherland** for "A Professional Beggar's Lullaby" from *Messages*, Africana Publishing Corp., NYC.

**Stella Ngatho** for "The Kraal" from *Poems From East Africa*, Africana Publishing Corp., NYC.

**Marjorie Oludhe-Macgoye** for "A Freedom Song" from *Poems From East Africa*, Africana Publishing Corp., NYC.

**Jared Angira** for "No Coffin, No Grave" from *Silent Voices*, Africana Publishing Corp., NYC.

**Joseph Gatuiria** for "Kariuki" from *Poems From Africa*, New American Library, Inc., Ave of the Americas.

**Bahadur Tejani** for "Leaving the Country" from *Pulsations*, East Africa Literature Bureau, Nairobi, Kenya Box 30022.

**Burns B. Machobane** for "False Brothers" from *The Word is Here*, 1973, Doubleday & Co., Garden City, N.Y.

**Guy C.Z. Mhone** for "Ife Head" from *The Greenfield Review*, Greenfield Center, N.Y. 12833

**David Rubadiri** for "Saaka Crested Cranes" from *Drumbeat*, East Africa Publishing, Makerere U. Kampala, Uganda.

**Chinua Achebe** from "Beware, Soul Brother" and "Mango Seedling" from *Christmas In Biafra*, Doubleday & Co., Garden City, N.Y.

**J.P. Clark** for "Night Rain" from *A Reed In The Tide*, 1965, Longman's & Green Co., 48 Grosvernor St., London WI, England.

**R.N. Egudu** for "The First Yam of the Year" from *The Literary Review, 1969.*

**Ifeanyi Menkiti** for "All Quiet on Slave Row" from *Chelsea*, P.O. Box 5880, Grand Central Station 10017.

**Ossie O. Enekwe** for "To A Friend Made and Lost in War" from *Okike*, Chinua Achebe, Ed. English Dept. University of Nigeria, Nsukka, Nigeria.

**Onwuchekwa Jemie** for "Iroko" from *Voyage*, 1971 Pan African Pocket Poets, Ulli Beier, University of Ife, Nigeria.

**Emmanuel Obiechina** for "Homecoming" from *Locusts*, The Greenfield Review Press, Greenfield Center, N.Y. 12833.

**Tanure Ojaide** for "Children of Iroko" and "The Kola of Life" from *Children of Iroko*, The Greenfield Review Press, Greenfield Center, N.Y. 12833.

**Gabriel Okara** for "One Night at Victoria Beach" from *Modern Poetry from Africa*, ed. by Moore and Beier, 1963, Penguin Books.

**Dennis Osadebey** for "Young Africa's Plea" from *Poems from Africa,* edited by Samuel Allen, Sutherland Rd., Brookline, Mass.

**Niyi Osundare** for "Eyekaire" and "A Wife's Complaint" from *The Greenfield Review,* Greenfield Center, N.Y. 12833.

**Mabel Imoukhuede Segun** for "The Pigeon Hole" from *New Voices of the Commonwealth,* Evans Brothers Ltd., Montague House, Russell Sq., London WC 1, England.

**Wole Soyinka** for "I Think it Rains" and "Telephone Conversation"

**Ken Tsaro-Wiwa** for "Voices".

**Kalu Uka** for "Fear" and "Earth to Earth" from *Earth to Earth,* The Greenfield Review Press, Greenfield Center, N.Y. 12833.

**Mamman J. Vatsa** for "Eagles", "Prayers of the Commonwealth" and "An African Spectator" from *The Greenfield Review,* Greenfield Center, N.Y. 12866.

**Okogbule Wonodi** for "Lament of the Exiles" from *Dusts of Exile,* Pam African Pocket Poets, 1971. Ulli Beier, Ife, Nigeria.

**Syl Cheney Coker** for "Volcano" from *The Greenfield Review,* Greenfield Center, N.Y 12833 and "Concerto for and Exile", from Africana Publishing Corp., NYC.

**Delphine King** for "The Child" from *New Voices from the Commonwealth,* Evans Brothers Ltd., Montague House, Russell Sq., London, WC 1, England.

**Abioseh Nicl** for "The Meaning of Africa".

**Dennis Brutus** for "Nightsong City" and "From Poem" from *Sirens, Knuckles, Boots,* 1963, Mbari, Ibadan.

**Zweli Ed Dladla** for "Epitaph on Faces" from *The Word is Here,* edited by Keorapetse Kgositsile, 1973, Doubleday.

**C.J. Driver** for "Elegy for My Contemporaries" from *Seven South African Poets,* Africana Publishing Corp., 101 5th Ave., NYC 10003.

**Timothy Holmes** for "The Conquered" and "Reaction to Conquest" from *Seven South African Poets,* Africana Publishing Corp., 101 5th Ave., NYC 10003.

**Keropatse Kgositsile** for "My People No Longer Sing" and "Yes Mandela" from *Seven South African Poets,* Africana Publishing Corp., 101 5th Ave., NYC 10003.

**Bloke Modisane** for "Lonely" from *Modern Poetry from Africa,* 1963 Peguin Books, 3300 Clipper Mill Rd., Baltimore, Maryland 21211.

**Ezekiel Mphahlele** for "Vingettes".

**C.D. Noble** for "Who is the Rain".

**Oswald Mtshali** for "Amagoduka at Glencoe Station" from *Songs of a Cowhide Drum,* The Third Press, Joseph Okpaku Publishing Co., 444 Central Part West, NYC 10025.

**Arthur Nortje** for "Waiting" and "Windscape" from *The Greenfield Review,* Greenfield Center, N.Y. 12833.

**Sydney Sipho Sepamla** for "Silence" and "Pigeon Holes" from *To Whom It May Concern,* South Africa.

**Mongane W. Serote** for "Death Survey", "A Wish to Lie Down" and "A Poem on Black and White" from *Tsetlo,* South Africa.

**Sarjo Datta** for "The Dead Bird" from *Poems From East Africa,* Africana Publishing Corp., 101 5th Ave., NYC 10003.

**Okot P. Bitek** for "Oasis" from *The Greenfield Review,* Greenfield Center, N.Y. 12833.

**Rose Mbowa** for "Ruin" from *New Voices of the Commonwealth,* Evans Brothers Ltd., Montague House, Russell Sq., London WC 1, England.

**U Win Pe** for "A Time to Tie the Mind" and "Poem for Wazo".

**G.S. Sharat Chandra** for "Second Journey", "Bharata Natyam Dancer", "The Black Deity" and "Bangla (Water Pipe) Desh.".

**Jyotirmoy Datta** for "Parting by the River" and "Treacherous Objects".

**Adil Jussawalla** for "Missing Person".

**Arun Kolatkar** for "The Railroad Station".

**Shiv K. Kumar** for "Aftermath" and "A Barren Woman".

**Arvind Krishna Mehrotra** for "Kabir's Last Entry", "A Dead Man Looks at Three Things" and "Songs of the Ganga".

**Jayanta Mahapatra** for "Down" and "The Whore House in a Calcutta Street".

**D. Parameswaran** for "Untitled".

**Gieve Patel** for "Just Strain Your Neck", "The Arrogant Meditation", "Body Fears, Here I Stand" and "Audience".

**A. K. Ramanujan** for "An Chan" and "Homecoming".

**Wong May** for "Study of a Millionairess: Still Life" from *New Voices of the Commonwealth*, 1968, Evans Brothers, Ltd., Montague House, Russell Sq., London, WC 1, England.

**Zulifkàr Ghose** for "Egypt" from *Commonwealth Poem of Today*, Evans Brothers, Ltd., Montague House, Russell Sq., Londong, WC 1, England.

**Shahid Hosain** for "Wedding".

**Maki Kureishi** for "The Fire Temple", "Statue of Bramha" and "Shall We drown the Kittens".

**Kaleem Omar** for "Karachi", "Monkeys at Hardwar", "Coming Down From the Mountains" and "5000 Years of Pakistan".

**Michael Ondaatje** for "Martinique" and "Prometheus, With Wings".

**Edward Brathwaite** for "Ogun" from *Islands* by Edward Brathwaite, Oxford University Press, Amen House, London, EC 4, England. Reprinted by permission of the author. And for "Columbus" from the *Emigrants*.

**Frank A. Collymore** for "This Land" and "Hymn to the Sea" from *The Blue Horizons*, Evans Brothers, Ltd., Montague House, Russell Sq., London, WC 1, England.

**A.N. Forde** for "Canes by the Roadside" from *The Blue Horizons*, Evans Brothers, Ltd., Montague House, Russell Sq., London, WC 1, England.

**Margaret Gill** for "Lovesong of a Canecutter" from *Savacou*, Dept. of History, University of West Indies, Kingston 7, Jamaica.

**Bruce St. John** for "Upstairs" and "Lighters"

**H.A. Vaughan** for "For Certain Demagogues" from *The Blue Horizons*, Evans Brothers, Ltd., Montague House, Russell Sq., London, WC 1, England.

**G. Charles** for "Song of the Cave Spirits".

**Royston Ellis** for "In the Gentle Afternoon" and "In the Shade of Our Heritage" from *New Writings From the Caribbean*, A. J. Seymore, Georgetown, Guyana.

**Syl Lowhar** for "The Colonial" from *Breaklight*, edited by Andrew Salkey, Hamish Hamilton Ltd., 90 Great Russell St., London, WC 1B3, England.

**Kwame Apata** for "Name Change" and "Pam Man" from *New Writings from The Caribbean*, A.J. Seymour, Georgetown, Guyana.

**Martin Carter** for "Cuyuni" from *New Writings From the Caribbean*, A.J. Seymour, Georgetown, Guyana.

**Roy Heath** for "The Wake" from *New Writings From the Caribbean*, A.J. Seymour, Georgetown Guyana.

**Shana Yardan** for "Earth is Brown" from *New Writings From the Caribbean*, A.J. Seymour, Georgetown, Guyana.

**Louise Bennett** for "Colonialization in Reverse", "Back to Africa", "Non Lickle Twang", "Colour-Bar" from *Jamaica Labrish*, Collins & Sengster, Ltd., Kingston, Jamaica.

**Bongo Jerry** for "Sooner or Later" from *Savacou*, Dept. of History, University of West Indies, Kingston 7, Jamaica.
**Gloria Escoffery** for "Guyanese Reflections".
**A.L. Hendriks** for "Mare Nostrum" from *Madonna of the Unknown Nation*, **Edward Lucie-Smith** for "The Hymn Tunes".
**Tony NcNeil** for "Straight Seeking" from *Breaklight*, edited by Andrew Salkey, Hamish Hamilton, Ltd., 90 Russell St., London, WC 1B3, England.
**Andrew Salkey** for "Postcard from Jamaica" and "Postcard from London" from *New Letters*, Editor David Ray, Univ. of Missouri, 5346 Charlotte, Kansas City, Missouri 64110.
**Dennis Scott** for "Epitaph", "Third World Blues", "Tom Tom" and "Exile" from *Breaklight*, edited by Andrew Salkey, Hamish Hamilton, Ltd., 90 Russell St., London, WC 1B3, England.
**Robert Lee** for "Return" from *The Greenfield Review*, Greenfield Center, N.Y. 12833.
**Derek Walcott** for "A Patriot to Patriots" from *New Writings From the Caribbean*, A.J. Seymour, Georgetown, Guyana.
**Elliott Bastien** from "Upside-Down Hotel" from *Breaklight*, edited by Andrew Salkey, Hamish Hamilton, Ltd., 90 Great Russell St., London England.
**Wayne Brown** for "Rasta Fisherman" from *Breaklight*, edited by Andrew Salkey, Hamish Hamilton, Ltd., 90 Great Russell St., London, England.
**Faustin Charles** for "Sugar Cane" and "Calypsonian" from *Breaklight*, edited by Andrew Salkey, Hamish Hamilton, Ltd., 90 Great Russell St., London, WC 1B3, England.
**Frank John** for "Husa" from *Breaklight*, edited by Andrew Salkey, Hamish Hamilton, Ltd., 90 Great Russell St., London, WC 1B3, England.
**Ian McDonald** for "Colour Poem" from *New Writings From the Caribbean*, A.J. Seymour, Georgetown, Guyanna and "Jaffo, the Calypsonian" from *Breaklight*, edited by Andrew Salkey, Hamish Hamilton, Ltd., 90 Great Russell St., London, WC 1B3, England.
**Jagdip Maraj** for "Faded Beauty" from *Breaklight*, edited by Andrew Salkey, Hamish Hamilton, Ltd. 90 Great Russell St., London, WC 1B3, England.
**Alvin Massy** for "Islands" from *The Greenfield Review*, Greenfield Center, N.Y. 12833.

In all cases every effort has been made to contact the authors whose poems have been used. Unless otherwise indicated, copyright for the individual poems remains in the name of the author and any requests to reprint any of the material included in this anthology should be made directly to the individual authors.

Publication of this book has been made possible by small press grants from New York State Council on the Arts, and the National Endowment for the Arts.

Cover photograph for *Aftermath* by Mary Ann Lynch ©1977.

**Special acknowledgement and thanks to Carol Bruchac for her continued work in the production and publication of *Aftermath*.**

# TABLE OF CONTENTS

# AFRICA

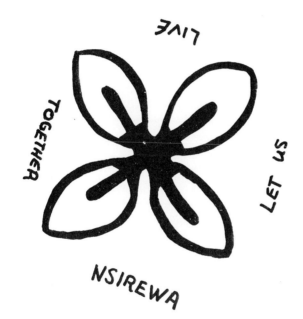

LIVE
TOGETHER
LET US
NSIREWA

# INTRODUCTION TO ANGLOPHONE POETRY
## OF WEST & SOUTH AFRICA

*by Ossie Onuora Enekwe*

## WEST AFRICAN POETRY

Although a colonial language such as English may expand readership, it can lead to sloppiness and lack of authenticity. Nevertheless, many anglophone West African writers have, as Chinua Achebe, chosen to transform the English language so that it is both in "full communion with its ancestral home" and is capable of carrying the weight of African experience. But since each writer must come to terms with the problem in his own way, the results are numerous and varied.

West African poetry in English began during the post-war (Second World War) era. It was strongly modelled after Christian hymns, and influenced by political slogans that thrived during the independence struggles. Usually naive and sentimental in content, and, thanks to its obsession with rhyme, stilted in syntax and rhythm, the pioneer poetry seems to lack artistic virtue, and is depreciated by the new generation of West African poets. Dennis Osadebay's "Young Africa's Plea," an embodiment of both the virtues and faults of the past, shows what recent poetry has gained or lost. The naive optimism has been superseded by a tough objectivity which sometimes borders on pessimism. Unfortunately, simplicity of diction has sometimes given way to obscurity.

Many of the present generation of poets are graduates of institutions of higher learning modelled after those in Britain. Having acquired formal education in the Humanities, these poets brought to their art a high sense of aesthetic concern. Their poetry is usually marked by eclecticism, juxtaposition of African and European cultural elements, predilection for abstract thought, and a morbid self-introspection that may be related to the pessimism of the twentieth-century European poetry. Pessimism may have been induced by a too close indentification with the social problems in the poets' own countries, for they believe that poetry can make things happen or change. A number of these writers have consequently suffered or died fighting for change. For instance, Wole Soyinka was imprisoned by Nigerian authorities for allegedly working for the rebels in the Biafra war, while Christopher Okigbo died fighting for Biafra.

Ambivalence is another quality of this poetry. Although these poets are inheritors of significant values of Europe, they are, emotionally at least, attached to their African roots. Kofi Awoonor, for instance, continues to use the form of the oral poetry of the Ewes of Ghana, partly because of a "desire to give this much neglected poetry a voice and to bring into focus the theme of cultural contact, conflict, and resolution for the modern African."

This belief in the validity of African cultures is the main impulse behind the extensive use by these poets of traditional elements, and the seemingly sentimental expression of nostalgia for the African past. Beyond laments about the destruction of African values, some writers, while observing and criticizing the European and American values, confidently assert the humanity and dignity of African cultures. Kofi Awoonor writes of "Harlem, the dark dirge of America." The "Telephone Conversation," by Wole Soyinka, is an acrid, but witty, attack on British racism.

But West African poets are not merely reactive. Moreover, they are highly individualistic, not communalistic, as many readers might expect. They are very much concerned with experimentation. However, despite its high aesthetic sense, the present generation of English-speaking West African poets has often been criticized for its obscurity. Some poets have responded to this criticism with a firm argument that simplicity is not a poetic virtue, that poetry demands mental effort. The debate about the nature of poetry is still on. However, the poems featured in this anthology seem to proclaim that clarity is a virtue.


SOUTH AFRICAN POETRY

In South Africa there is a strong tradition of oral poetry, initially idyllic and apolitical, and subsequently, as a result of the break down of tribal life, epical. The later mode deals with African heroes such as Chaka the Zulu. In written form, the epic mode carries the weight of the black-white racial tension which has been nurtured by Pretoria. Modern South African poetry in English is rooted in the present, in the reality such as Soweto where blacks are systematically dehumanized and destroyed. This poetry can easily become raucous. Fortunately, this is not common. Aware of the rage in his heart, the average South African poet does not take it for granted; he controls it.

This attempt to control his anger is not an obligation to "the republic of letters." It stems from a genuine need to transform this human emotion into something liberating and meaningful for both blacks and whites. Ezekiel Mphahlele points out that bitterness is not inherently anti-art. The

3

works of Dennis Brutus, Arthur Nortje, Mazisi Kunene and others prove him right. Their embattled verses are almost always suffused with tenderness and love.

If the South African regime remains deaf to love songs, it may soon reap a rich harvest of violence, for black Africans may soon change their tunes. Time is running out. In fact, it is surprising that South African poets are still talking searching for love, even though "the amplitude of sentiment" has brought them no nearer to anything affectionate.

While their West African counterparts may discuss the need for writers to keep a good distance from social crisis, South African poets are forced to be involved, and achieve self-definition in action.

Many of the leading South African poets are in exile. Although exile permits a degree of aesthetic distance, it also creates, as Arthur Nortje has noted, "the radiation burns of silence," and even worse, a sense of rootlessness that is the bane of even the most committed artists.

South African poetry is an enigma to those who are allergic to revolutionary art, for despite its dedication to liberty, it is not deficient in beauty and humanity.

*Cameroon*
Mbella Sonne Dipoko

## EXILE

In silence
The overloaded canoe leaves our shores

But who are these soldiers in camouflage,
These clouds going to rain in foreign lands?

The night is losing its treasures
The future seems a myth
Warped on a loom worked by lazy hands.

But perhaps all is not without some good for us
As from the door of a shack a thousand miles away
The scaly hand of a child takes in greeting
The long and skinny fingers of the rain.

# OUR LIFE

An ailing bird over the desert made its agony
A song blown through the air
As at the oasis
Drawers of water said
How low it flies oh how touching its song

The winged hope that proved to be a dream
(Masked our destiny with a black hood)

As in the cities we said the same prayers
As in the villages we espoused ancestral myths
Transmitting our frustration our life our mortality
To the young country of tomorrow and day after tomorrow
Flattering ourselves with the charity of the blood-donor's
    love.

Parachute men say
The first jump
Takes the breath away
Feet in the air disturb
Till you get used to it.

Solid ground
Is not where you left it
As you plunge down
Perhaps head first

As you listen to
Your arteries talking
You learn to sustain hope.

Suddenly you are only
holding an umbrella
In a windy place
As the warm earth
Reaches out to you
Reassures you
The vibrating interim is over.

You try to land
Where green grass yields
And carry your pack
Across the fields

The violent arrival
Puts out the joint
Earth has nowhere to go
You are at the starting point

Jumping across worlds
In condensed time
After the awkward fall
We are always at the starting point

*Ghana*
G. Adali-Mortty

## VILLAGE NIGHTS

Fearsome and dark are village nights!
How odd of me
To near-forget those village nights.
Here, seen through baccy smoke
The spectred looming gloom
Here, in Aloka, harrowed by the hush,
Reminds me.

The only voice a cricket's
Chirp-chirping from the rice that's wet, so wet,
Standing all its life in swamp.
Village nights are not like city nights so bright,
So companioned and so safe from haunting gnomes.
Village nights are different.
Dark, so dark and dank.
I'd half-forgot the pitch, the blinding pitch
Of nights of childhood and of youth.
As man I thought 'twas fancy
Made me fear the darkness
Of the nights at Gbogame
The village of my birth.

There, behind each hillock, tree or bush,
Stalk imaginables various,
Whining, groaning, moaning, sighing;
Nymphs, goblins, arrow-carrying dwarfs
In every wood.  They vied with us
Collecting berries.  They envied
Us, the children of humans.
They spoilt our play, and licked our soup.

Where are they, the spirits of the night?
Where? Here, Aloka nights repeat
The nights my village knew:
My childhood's nights so dark!

Ama Ata Aidoo

## CORNFIELDS IN ACCRA

They told us
Our mothers told us
They told us.

They told us
Our fathers told us
They told us.

They told us
Red clay
Will shine,
Shine silica,
Shine gold
Red clay will shine

It will shine
Where you polish
How-when-where
You polish.

They told us
Our mothers told us
They told us.

And so
We planted our corn:
Not whole seeds from
Last year's harvest
No,
For we are men without barns
Women without fallows.

Greased and petrolled earth,
Bits of tyres, really
All types of scrap-metal.

Some said,
Referring to the corn-seeds,
"They come from Russia"
Others that the bags were marked
"Nigeria."
But we have refused to listen
Or hearing,
Have not cared.

For
When Yaa looked over her courtyard and saw Akosua's
daughter passing by with her trayful of red clay that
shone and gleamed, did she not beg a mould?
And did she wait until she knew which pit had yielded the clay?

They told us
Our mothers told us
They told us.

And we thought
As we fixed the pipe—
They said it will carry
50,000 cc. of water every day—
We thought
As we fixed the pipe,
"The first day it rains
We shall plant
The corn."

Plot One
Was Nikoi's

It was at the backyard
Where once stood the fitter's
shop:
There,
Among skeleton cars,

The rest,
Hmm, brother,
Was less, not more
Dignified.
Mine was by a mango tree,
A hillock of rubbish dump
A deserted vacant-lot,
With unmentionable contents of diverse chamber-pots.

Yet
Even now
When that moon has not fully died
Which rose on our planting,
Let us sing of
Dark green wavy corn.

My brother,
My sister,
Take the refrain,
Swell the chorus,

They told us
Our mothers told us
They told us.

Finally,
When we have harvested, gleaned and
Threshed our corn,
Or roasted it aromatic,

That is,
After office hours
On Saturdays and throughout the whole of Sunday,
We shall sit firmly on our bottoms
And plant our feet on the earth,

Then
We shall ask to see
Him

Who says
We
Shall not survive among these turbines.

Who
Says
We shall not survive among the turbines?

Jawa Apronti

# FUNERAL

At home Death claims
Two streams from women's eyes
And many day-long dirges;
Gnashes, red eyes and sighs from men,
The wailing of drums and muskets
And a procession of the townsfolk
Impeded        .
Only if the coffin decides
To take one last look at the home.

But here I see
Three cars in procession.
The first holds three —
A driver chatting gaily with a mate,
And behind them, flowers on a bier.
The second holds five, and the third too.

A procession
Efficiently arranged by the undertaker,
From the brass fittings on the bier
To the looks of sorrow on the mourners' faces.
And Death is escorted
Tearlessly but efficiently
By
Three cars in procession.

## AFRO-AMERICAN BEATS

i.
Feet fall, jiving man
trailing beat and arguments of impossibility
conga drums and tom-toms in Apollo:
Nina Simone and Roberta Flack are getting it together,
doing their thing, shedding this earth of putrescent plutonic light
letting in the black breeze of the warm south.

ii.   *To Maya Angelou*

Maya baby, I read your book
of caged-birds, and my tummy was filled
with birds flying southwards and
to Africa, to river gods and ancestral shrines,
your Arkansas youth was the mystery
of earth and the wine bursting forth in blood and balls
jazz and blues in basements
evangelical hymns and father clocks
dim versions of our lineage here
where you and I are captives of time.
I remember you as Mother Courage,
large savanna princess with the voice of thunder
dragging your wagon of pain across the dying gut of Africa.

iii.   *An American Memory of Africa*

Black as my night, anonymous here
my death in Elizabethville was your death.
Blood shed in Sharpeville was shed before in Ulundi
Alabama, Memphis
Fred Hampton on a Chicago bed
blood and gun fire in darkness

was it prophesied that the panther
shall die in his bed without a leap?
I hug my black skin here against my better judgement
hung my shields and sheaves for a season
Leaving Africa that September 1967
in flight from the dreams we build
in the pale talons of eagles yard
donkeys braying on the bloody field across the square
the bulge of my sails unfurl for the
harbor ,of hate;
The pride of this color
by which they insist on defining my objection;
that I am a nigger is no matter
but that I died in Memphis and Elizabethville
outrages my self-esteem
I plot my vengeance silently
like Ellison's men in bright dens
of hiding and desperate anonimity
and with the hurricanes and eagles of tomorrow
prepare a firm and final rebuttal to your lies.
To be delivered in the season of infinite madness.


iv.   *To Langson Hughes When He Walked Among Us In Kampala,*
      *1962*


To that gathering of wooden headed boys
you came, pops, singing your jazz solos
in whiskied nights,
black nativity for Rome, raisins in the sun
For Harlem, bagmen of black rebirth
beats of drums jive talk
and her daddy-o singing that song
"I wonder where I'm gonna die
being neither white nor black."
Your dusky rivers gurgling down your throat

watering fields for your soul
the rivers you've known
beneath slave ships
whip lashes
and the golden note
you heard the sweep of ancient rivers
and daddy-o you died in Harlem.


v.  *To the Anonymous Brown-skinned Girl in Fresno*

I remember your face distinctly
haunting serenity glistening teeth
eyes the passion of centuries
we exchanged polite conversation
You took me in your cadillac across town
to Oakland where pot-bellied papas
guard deserted storefronts,
there was the sting of tear gas
following the riots in the Berkeley air that May
broads and winos all over the place,
between periodic love making
you outlined your revolutionary dreams
your coming trip to Algiers,
the smell of afterlove
and spent weary pubic aroma
when at once the light shone from your dark beautiful soul
and I knew who you were.

vi.
Hold on there, the rag man
half-assed jiving mother
celebrant in rented tuxedo
barker at others' carnivals
for barren pennies you will vomit blood
and asphalt here in speaking to police dogs

and night sticks on the outskirts of Harlem;
my friend, pimp for downtown rich
limping from cudgel wounds
broken torso, black tooth jack-anapes
even the hairs in your ass-hole have been eaten by termites.
Remember what Malcolm said when you asked a dumb question?

vii.  *Characteristic Leaders*

Charlie Parker, Coltrane
the true artists of a battered age
must take a trip; to draw cards
all true prophets must lose their voice;
for now the sanguine moon pale across my doorway
is singing in my bathroom
intricate fabrics woven in your trombonic voice
John the Baptist and the bird of paradise,
despised angel of infinite mercy
who made his nest in Newport
only to be despoiled.  What happened
to the real voice of Miles before he abandoned
heavenly sounds for the vibrations of electricity
and jived doped rock bullshit?
When be-bop was born on hilly grounds,
these imitators were wriggling to the braying of donkeys
others were needed to keep their ears to earth
to hear the footfalls, and the beat, and crack
and vibes of mother's heart
across ten thousand years of our primal nakedness.

Kwesi Brew

## THE DIRGE

I was talking to a girl at the well
When they came to tell me
The sun has fallen
On the leaves.
Behind the forest.
I picked up my gourd
And went my way!

At home,
Adoma was treading waist-beads,
For her red passion cloth.
One by one, she clicked
One by one, for the loved one.
My wife sat by herself
All alone,
Spinning and singing.

The storm shouted
And his brother lightning
Smote down the door!
There was none to stop them, then.
They followed, the evil ones
They followed,
Followed me
Like wiry hunting dogs
With the glaze of the burning bush
On the ridges of their tongues.

They came
Dry and keen-eyed
And told her
There will be decades of nights.

Till one day
When the gods please

There will be
Day again.
Because,
The sun has fallen
On the leaves
Behind the forest
And the stars are coming down
In dust and ashes.


## ANCESTRAL FACES

They sneaked into the limbo of time,
But could not muffle the gay jingling
Bells on the frothy necks
Of the sacrificial sheep
That limped and nodded after them.
They could not hide the moss on the bald pate
Of their reverent heads,
And the gnarled bark of the wawa tree;
Nor the rust on the ancient state-swords
Nor the skulls studded with grinning cowries.
They could not silence the drums,
The fibre of their souls and ours—
The drums that whisper to us behind black sinewy
       hands.
They gazed and
Sweeping like white locusts through the forests
Saw the same men, slightly wizened,
Shuffle their sandalled feet to the same rhythms.
They heard the same words of wisdom uttered
Between puffs of pale blue smoke.
They saw us,
And said!  They have not changed!

Joe De Graft

# THE OLD SEA CHAIN

At the end of this slip-way,
Beyond the foaming breakers,
The old sailing ships used to rest
Preening their white wings in the breeze
As they waited for their cargo.

Look now, how the green sea-weed
Covers all the slip-way!

Now feel,
Feel with the sole of your infant feet
The fierce dragon rock beneath the silken weed,
Teeth-of-dragon rock stained red-brown
As with ancient blood —
Blood not all the waters of the sea can wash away.

Then look across the ocean;
Look beyond the breakers,
Far out beyond the curve
Of meeting sky and ocean,
And tell me what you see.

Nothing?

Yet in those ancestral days
There was a chain —
A chain of flesh and iron wrought;
And it held beyond this slip-way,
Reaching out to sea
Far, far beyond the curve
Of meeting sky and ocean,
On to the other side of the Atlantic.

Kojo Gyinaye Kyei

## AFRICAN IN LOUISIANA

I stopped deep
In Louisiana once,
A cop close at my heels:
What! *Go to the coloured side.*
*Don't sit here!*

Somewhat angry,
But indeed, hungry,
I could only say:
*Some day we will meet again,*
*Your heart changed*
*For friendship.*

I sat, though,
And was served soup
In a miracle-whip bottle
I still keep
For a keepsake.

## THE TALKING DRUMS

I hear the beat
of the drums,
The *Atumpan* drums,
Asante Kotoko:
*Kum-apem-a-apem-beba!*

I hear the beat
of Prempeh drums,
Osei Tutu drums.

I hear the call
of Nnawuta:
*Tinn-tinn konn-konn!*
*Tinn-tinn Konn-konn!*
*Konn-konn!*

I ponder the valour
Of the mourned and mighty
African might.
I sense the resonance
Of Dawuro beats:
*Tonn-tonn sann-sann!*
*Tonn-tonn sann-sann!*
*Sann-sann!*

I muse upon Ghana,
Melle and Songhay
I hear the echo
Of *Fontomfrom,*
The beat of
*Mpintin* drums:
*Damirifa due . . . due!*
*Damirifa due . . . due!*

I hear the beat
Of the drums!
' hear the beat
Of the Talking Drums!

Efua Sutherland

## A PROFESSIONAL BEGGAR'S LULLABY

Don't cry baby,
Son, at two years old
You'll be a prodigy beggar kid,
Cute wide-eyed toddler beggar
Outside United Nations;
On that swanky beat,
'Painy-painy' lisping
And thriving on the coming in
And going out of world distresses,
Don't cry baby.

Kofi Anyidoho

# FROM SOUL IN BIRTHWATERS
(Suite for the Revolution)


i.    Our Birth-Cord

        a piece of meat lost in cabbage stew
        it will be found        it will be found

If we must die at birth, pray
we return with our birth-cord still uncut
our oneness with Earth undefiled

Last night on the village square a man
bumped into my conscience and cursed
our god.  I refused to retort, knowing
how hard it is for man to wake a man
from false slumber
Our conscience would not be hurt
by threats of lunatics

        a pinch of salt lost in cabbage stew
        it will be found    the tongue will feel it out

We heard their cries but thought of dogs
and ghosts.  Ghosts gone mad at dogs
who would not give our village a chance
to sleep, to dream
Now they say we have to die
These brand-new men gone slightly drunk
on public wine they say we have to die

Yet if we must die at birth, pray
we return with our birth-cord still uncut
our name still to be found in the book of souls

Across the memory of a thousand agonies
our death shall gallop into the conference hall of a million hopes
a lone delegate at reshuffling of destinies

    a piece of hope lost in public tears
    it will be found     it will be found

And if we must die at birth, pray
we return with —
But we were not born to be killed
by threats of lunatics
The maimed panther is no playmate for antelopes

                12 Aug. 1975


ii.    <u>Radio Revolution</u>

Again this dawn our Radio
broke off the vital end of sleep

Revolution!...............Devolution!...............Resolution!

grab a razor-sharp matchet
and step onto the paths of war

Across our yard I disturbed a courtship of
the dogs. They barked and backed away

through streets to all familiar walks
through maze of slums to armed barracks
of peace. Where? Where?
old peasant with hoe in hand, I
seek Revolution. Where is Revolution?
young veteran with blood across blue eyes, I
knew of no Revolution, but I
met Revolt limping down this road
chased by a howling herd of armed jackals

down this road down this road
to the market square where an only
pig searching for a morning meal
took me for a moving lump of flesh
and charged at me charged at me
with fangs sharpened by hunger's despair

I slashed her into two, wiped her
blood upon
                her head

down this road     down this road
to Dependence Square seeking Revolution
I found a lone symbol for Peace
a nameless bronze warrior with empty
gun pointing earthwards doing homage
to earth goddess

The school-boy news-pedlar leans against
a smile tells of how he came and found my doors
open my inner rooms unguarded in the dawn

I was out my dear
I was out seeking Revolution

Our Revolution, Sir?  It's here in these
dailies.  The headlines display it:

THE REVOLUTION — NOT A CONCERT PARTY

The photographs confirm it:

Statesmen at State Banquets
Proposing a toast to the health of State:
LONG  LEAVE THE REVOLUTION!!!

Legon
5-7 Mar. 1976

26

*Kenya*
Stella Ngatho

## THE KRAAL

The kraal fence
    hides quarrels
Of jealous wives,
    it hides the miseries within
and sadness
    of wives fallen from favour.
It excludes anyone
    beyond its gate
That reed fence
    _spells laughter, joy
and happiness to the outside
    but hides the cruelty
of the husband within
    to the tortured tormented wife,
the sad one full of woes:
    the favoured one full of ease and joy.
Yes, that reed fence hides plenty.

Marjorie Oludhe-Macgoye

## A FREEDOM SONG

Atieno washes dishes,
Atieno plucks the chicken,
Atieno gets up early,
Beds her sacks down in the kitchen,
Atieno eight years old,
Atieno yo.

Since she is my sister's child
Atieno needs no pay,
While she works my wife can sit
Sewing every sunny day:
With her earnings I support
Atieno yo.

Atieno's sly and jealous,
Bad example to the kids
Since she minds them, like a schoolgirl
Wants their dresses, shoes and beads,
Atieno ten years old,
Atieno yo.

Now my wife has gone to study
Atieno is less free.
Don't I keep her, school my own ones,
Pay the party, union fee,
All for progress: aren't you grateful
Atieno yo?

Visitors need much attention,
All the more when I work night.
That girl spends too long at market.
Who will teach her what is right?

Atieno rising fourteen,
Atieno yo.

Ateino's had a baby
So we know that she is bad.
Fifty fifty it may live
And repeat the life she had
Ending in post-partum bleeding,
Atieno yo.

Atieno's soon replaced.
Meat and sugar more than all
She ate in such a narrow life
Were lavished on her funeral.
Atieno's gone to glory,
Atieno yo.

Jared Angira

## NO COFFIN, NO GRAVE

He was buried without a coffin
without a grave
the scavengers performed the post-mortem
in the open mortuary
without sterilized knives
in front of the night club

stuttering rifles put up
the gun salute of the day
that was a state burial anyway
the car knelt
the red plate wept, wrapped itself into blood its master's

the diary revealed to the sea
the rain anchored there at last
isn't our flag red, black, and white?
so he wrapped himself well

who could signal yellow
when we had to leave politics to the experts
and brood on books
brood on hunger
and schoolgirls
grumble under the black pot
sleep under torn mosquito net
and let lice lick our intestines
the lord of the bar, money speaks madam
woman magnet, money speaks madam
we only cover the stinking darkness
of the cave of our mouths
and ask our father who is in hell to judge him
the quick and the good.

Well, his diary, submarine of the Third World War
showed he wished
to be buried in a gold-laden coffin
like a VIP
under the jacaranda tree'beside his palace
a shelter for his grave
and much beer for the funeral party

anyway one noisy pupil suggested we bring
tractors and plough the land.

Joseph Gatuiria

## KARIUKI

The hour of midnight met with a gathering of mothers,
Their only talk—names upon names.
 "It will be my nephew" one said,
 "No, my sister's cousin." "Kirahiu
 Is the name or should it be Mwnagi?"

Then I heard the delicate squeal of a baby
 (It is of an hour's age)
Caused no less than a whole village to awake.
 What causes them to awake?
 And an old man comes struggling into the house.

"How are you, Kariuki?" This he whispers
To the deaf stranger of this world.
 Whereupon the "Kariuki" begins its endless journey.
 It floats from mouth to mouth
 "It's a boy?" "Kariuki is born!"
 The old warrior is born again.

Bahadur Tejani

## LEAVING THE COUNTRY

Then the mind
became a body
immersed
in the water blanket of monsoon
a deep daze of dislocation
from colour
and creed
and country.

The vague ache
of memories
that interspersed
space time
like some lost children
in the forest
unworried by strange roads
because everything is unknown

unafraid of twilight
because all
is the long evening
wandering because
the unsure step onward
is the fate
function of limbs.

Yet terrified because
the forest is endless
and outside
through a pale patch
of the green darkness
the sun shines
like a chimera
that deepens the
global gloom.

Only one solace:
there have been
others too,
lingering in that twilight,
who shed
home and country
and at times
colour
who travelled the long way
and also never felt happy.

*Lesotho*
Burns B. Machobane

## FALSE BROTHERS

Rap to 'em, brother
Tell 'em about the man
Tell 'em to git together
       United we stand
       Divided we fall

Rap to 'em
Tell 'em about Af'ica
Black is beautiful
       They got to be hip
       They got to be wise

Y'also gonna tell 'em
That Tarzan's Ole Lady
Is also your Broad
Or are you . . . still. . .
Just usin' 'em. . . Brother
       Rap to me!

*Malawi*
Guy C. Z. Mhone

## IFE HEAD

Why an ancestral nakedness
Thus exposed to them
Who spat on us
When you lay treasured in our soil
Below layers of generations
Of our dead.

Ife head, you stand there
Stone mute
Stripped and bare
No drums to beat
No tales to share
Mere stares of lust
Mediocre flattery at your past
They bestow on you

Here your tale we know
Hidden in the pen of our song
The communion of our feet/
                      with our dark soil
Our twitches of the muscle/
                      to tales of the drum
With you undug/
                      your nakedness unexposed
Ife head
Why an ancestral nakedness
Thus exposed to them.

David Rubadiri

## SAAKA CRESTED CRANES

The Prison Farm at Saaka
cradles craggy trucks
old and grey
on which pelicans perch;

Saaka they say
is a crater lake,
bottomless —
ringed with banana homes
the feminine complexity
of prison
and fertility;

It was in this water of life
as the children call it
that one evening
quiet and still
swooped a troop of crested cranes
Ngaali on the wing,

as we held hands,
swirling upwards
crested high
majestically borne
like priests of Osiris
to nest.

*Nigeria*
Chinua Achebe

## BEWARE, SOUL BROTHER

We are the men of soul
men of song we measure out
our joys and agonies
too, our long, long passion week
in paces of the dance. We have
come to know from surfeit of suffering
that even the Cross need not be
a dead end nor total loss
if we should go to it striding
the dirge of the soulful *abia* drums . . .
    But beware soul brother
of the lures of ascension day
the day of soporific levitation
on high winds of skysong; beware
for others there will be that day
lying in wait leaden-footed, tone-deaf
passionate only for the deep entrails-
of our soil; beware of the day
we head truly skyward leaving
that spoil to the long ravenous tooth
and talon of their hunger.
Our ancestors, soul brother, were wiser
than is often made out. Remember
they gave Ala, great goddess
of their earth, sovereignty too over
their arts for they understood
so well those hard-headed
men of departed dance where a man's
foot must return whatever beauties
it may weave in air, where
it must return for safety
and renewal of strength. Take care

then, mother's son, lest you become
a dancer disinherited in mid-dance
hanging a lame foot in air like the hen
in a strange unfamiliar compound. Pray
protect this patrimony to which
you must return when the song
is finished and the dancers disperse;
remember also your children
for they in their time will want
a place for their feet when
they come of age and the dance
of the future is born
for them.

## MANGO SEEDLING

Through glass window pane
Up a modern office block
I saw, two floors below, on wide-jutting
concrete canopy a mango seedling newly sprouted
Purple, two-leafed, standing on its burst
Black yolk. It waved brightly to sun and wind
Between rains—daily regaling itself
On seed-yams, prodigally.
For how long?
How long the happy waving
From precipice of rainswept sarcophagus?
How long the feast on remnant flour
At pot bottom?

Perhaps like the widow
Of infinite faith it stood in wait
For the holy man of the forest, shaggy-haired
Powered for eternal replenishment.
Or else it hoped for Old Tortoise's miraculous feast

On one ever recurring dot of cocoyam
Set in a large bowl of green vegetables—
This day beyond fable, beyond faith?
    Then I saw it
Poised in courageous impartiality
Between the primordial quarrel of Earth
And Sky striving bravely to sink roots
Into objectivity, mid-air in stone.

I thought the rain, prime mover
To this enterprise, someday would rise in power
And deliver its ward in delirious waterfall
Toward earth below.  But every rainy day
Little playful floods assembled on the slab,
Danced, parted round its feet,
United again, and passed.
It went from purple to sickly green
Before it died.
    Today I see it still—
Dry, wire-thin in sun and dust of the dry months—
Headstone on tiny debris of passionate courage.

John Pepper Clark

## NIGHT RAIN

What time of night it is
I do not know
Except that like some fish
Doped out of the deep
I have bobbed up bellywise
From stream of sleep
And no cocks crow.
It is drumming hard here
And I suppose everywhere
Droning with insistent ardour upon
Our roof-thatch and shed
And through sheaves slit open
To lightning and rafters
I cannot make out overhead
Great water drops are dribbling
Falling like orange or mango
Fruits showered forth in the wind
Or perhaps I should say so


Much like beads I could in prayer tell
Them on string as they break
In wooden bowls and earthenware
Mother is busy now deploying
About our roomlet and floor.
Although it is so dark
I know her practised step as
She moves her bins, bags, and vats
Out of the run of water
That like ants filing out of the wood
Will scatter and gain possession
Of the floor. Do not tremble then

But turn brothers, turn upon your side
Of the loosening mats
To where the others lie.

We have drunk tonight of a spell
Deeper than the owl's or bat's
That wet of wings may not fly.
Bedraggled upon the *iroko*, they stand
Emptied of hearts, and
Therefore will not stir, no, not
Even at dawn for then
They must scurry in to hide.
So we'll roll over on our back
And again roll to the beat
Of drumming all over the land
And under its ample soothing hand
Joined to that of the sea
We will settle to sleep of the innocent.

R. N. Egudu

## THE FIRST YAM OF THE YEAR

I have dug it fresh,
this boneless flesh
of air, earth, warmth
and water, this
life out of the heart
of death;
its cap of fibre
will mail the elder's
head against grey rain,
and its body proof his
to spite time's arrows.

For his is the rope
tied at the foot
of our past hooking
its fingers round our waist,
and reaching for the sable
gourd on the forked stump
where the unfeathered chick
chirps a sacrificial song.

He will eat this log-root
of earth, and after spread
my skin under the Red-Sun
to collect his rays
for washing my blood,
and plant the ageless
sun-tree into my heart.

Ifeanyi Menkiti

## ALL QUIET ON SLAVE ROW

                    Nor could they tell
                    whether the Ne-
                    gro was of Man
                    or was somewhere
                    between an ant-
                    elope and a man.

We danced on the ephemera,
the ephemera danced with us,
us and the ephemera were one.

Lord of joy
and intermingled blessedness;

Jerusalem was builded there,
among the dark-set sea.

Arabs came;
the Jews before them.

But, here, in our authentic
southern sea, we wept

and spat the seeds
of watermelon —

jolly niggers
come to town.

And there was this adult pain
down deep in the soul

because of which
was laughter.

Lord of tears
and perspiratory blessedness,

we shook, we shook
to the rhythm of juba.

*Nigeria*
Ossie O. Enekwe

# TO A FRIEND MADE AND LOST IN WAR

God had saved you
at Ihiala, Ozubulu
and Eluama where you lay
on the tracks of enemy guns.
But a hungry driver
and a tired truck
hauled you into a ditch
in a thick bush.
Blood oozed from your nose,
mouth and ears;
and at a village hospital
where they nursed you,
"God may get tired
of saving me," you said
to me, a smile on your lips.

Two days later,
Soviet bomber rockets
burst your belly
and tore your intestine
on the white sheet
of the hospital bed.
Slowly your life spread
purple about you.
They bore you weeping
to another place
and tried to stitch you,
to keep your soul
from escaping in the purple flow.
But you had too many holes.

So you died among strangers.
We could not find you.
We came too late to the morgue,
and too late to see you buried.
We could not tell
from the many mounds
which was yours,
since the grave diggers
had left for the weekend,
after a tiring week.
They must have let you drop
like cargo in the hold of a ship.
We could tell how tired
they must have been
from the half-covered pits.

We could not have
dug you out for a better pit.
We only wanted to identify your portion
and stand over you awhile,
at least to prove to you
that you had friends.


BROKEN POTS


The heavy bosomed hill
Lies close to our hut
And the winding narrow path
Stumbles into our farm.

Up above where the squirrels prance
Or the naughty little birds twitter
About my little sister and me
I want to go and see
The king of the animals.

At night when the cold wind
Runs its fingers through our bodies
Like a drunken lover,
We want to press close to our mother
To break off the crawling touch.

We always hear, soft and clear,
Like the wail of a lost lamb,
The voice of a virgin
Whose pot of water
Has slipped and crumbled
While its little fountain
Lingers into our farm.

Many have cried
And I have heard many varied voices:
Husky ones as people who eat too much corn,
Muted ones like sighs from broken hearts,
And others which, because I'm too young,
I cannot name.

But I know that some
When they wreck their glory
Within the shades of a benign bush
Never cry as when the pot breaks.

Onwuchekwa Jemie

## LAMENT OF THE EXILES

I

Come sit with me among my own
Under thatched roof
And shelter your hair
From the noonday heat, from dust and rain.

Sit with me and we'll spread our hands
Around fires and talk of gods
That haunt houses
And walk among men as friends.

We will talk of midnight kings, chiefs and VIPs,
Of glistering palaquins beside mud houses;
I will sing tales of nocturnal offerings
And the days of blood that followed

Mocking the prophecies of medicinemen
That the dead come back wiser than they left;
For the eyes of my people grow red
And the people see red blood on the roofs.

Emmanuel Obiechina

## HOME — COMING

We plunged in medias res
Into the septic belly of our afflictions,
Savoured every delicate agony,
Weighed every dram of pain,
And sucked the nectar of despair
From the poisoned flower
Of the tree of death.

Where were our homes
Where once we romped as children?
Where our birthday palms, the umbilical cords
Chaining our birth to our earth,
Our earth to our eternity?
Where were the ancestral hearths
Where the living and the dead
Supped in concord?

We surprised a wailing home,
A land scorched with fire;
Confronted a snowfield of whitening bones,

II

We returned to beheaded homes
Where beheaded trees stood like bemused
Sentinels over blackened desolation;
All life stood beheaded, becalmed,
In the trapped silence
Of beheaded winds.

Our anguished eyes swept backward
Into the mutilated innards
Of our ravished homeland.
We saw again the blazing inferno
Sweep over the wracked and raped land,
The trees trembling and forlorn,
Birds, goats, sheep, dogs and chicken
Waiting in muted sadness
The final spasms of their death agony

We saw the majestic python
The silvery totem of the clan
In tearful retreat,
Abandoñ the sacred grove
and tutelary care of the land;
We saw the outraged gods
In mournful procession
Leave their shrines
In the wake of their fleeing worshippers:


### III

Idemili, Amadiora, Dimudeke, Ani,
Olisaebuluwa,
Sad-eyes refugees, dumbstruck exiles,
Uneasily squatting in thin acre
On resentful godland.

We saw again
That once beautiful land,
Earth that sprang green grass
And trees that bore fruit,
Birds that chattered in the trees,
Flooding the sunrise with heady birdsong;
We saw kids frollicking in the sand

Men kindling the fagoots of far-flaming hopes,
Whose gaiety subdued the headiest wines;
We saw that fair and fruitful land
Ground dead and silent
Under the iron hooves of overweaning power.

Yet, as we stood with sunken hearts
And horror-scoured souls,
Looking upon the scourged, murdered land,
The lesson of history, like a bud
Openingly smilingly into the morning sun,
Revived our numbed senses:
There is no end to the mystery
Of life and death.


## IV

Life is perpetually renewed
Beyond the dust and ashes
Of death and desolation.
Upon the wasteland of a dead universe,
Rain will fall again,
Earth shall renew itself, pulsating
New warmth, and zest and life:
Earth stands perpetually dead
And perennially renewed.

Tanure Ojaide

## CHILDREN OF IROKO

Now acolyte, you must dress new
In white calico with red bands,
Like the Virgin priestess
A feather-hat from forest birds
And lead the procession on.

Carry them on:
Newly baked serrated chalk
A white cock without a crow
Three-lobed kolanuts
Seven half-pennies
Put them on the white plate, carry
Them on towards the happy shrine
And let the cow be led behind. . .

A year is gone past
After rains, harvests and suns,
Hairs have gone more grey without
New entrance to the grave-fields,
Women have groaned, not for grief
But in begetting more sons
And children are saved from pythons
And puff-adders.

Now is the new moon
Crescent favourable:
Dry tumulus at the right hand
Lacks libation wine to flourish.
He needs a cow, a milky cow
Send a herald to announce
    Protective prayers
    Fecundive rites
    And happy thanks. . .

Acolyte, the priestess by your right
Place the weighty carriage on the floor
And touch your forehead on the ground.
Pour the wine
　　in drops;
　　　　Let it stream
　　　　　over the ground
　　　　　　to sink beneath
And let Ononobrughwe take his fill. . .
"You show you love us
We kneel before you and for you
We thank you."
Fast and fast, beat loud the drums
Back to begin a new year.


THE KOLA OF LIFE

Nobody bars weakness with cement blocks.

When a couple makes love in the Botanical Garden
The Landlord expels them from their paradise
And dawn hides the exiles in a brush—
Prophetic truth frightens the unprepared incumbent
As spokes of fire embarrass who live in darkness.

The Berlin Wall separates us. . .

A corn infested sole walks a roughly gravelled road
Children whose mother is gone to market are crying
The only child whose mother is dead is playing
A vital sacrifice reinstates our losses.

Granny, split for me the kola of life
May the lobes rearrange my mind.

Gabriel Okara

# ONE NIGHT AT VICTORIA BEACH

The wind comes rushing from the sea,
the waves curling like mambas strike
the sands and recoiling hiss in rage
washing the Aladuras' feet pressing hard
on the sand and with eyes fixed hard
on what only hearts can see, they shouting
pray, the Aladuras pray; and coming
from booths behind, compelling highlife
forces ears; and car lights startle pairs
arm in arm passing washer-words back
and forth like haggling sellers and buyers—

Still they pray, the Aladuras pray
with hands pressed against their hearts
and their white robes pressed against
their bodies by the wind; and drinking
palmwine and beer, the people boast
at bars at the beach. Still they pray.

They pray, the Aladuras pray
to what only hearts can see while dead
fishermen long dead with bones rolling
nibbled clean by nibbling fishes, following
four dead cowries shining like stars
into deep sea where fishes sit in judgement;
and living fishermen in dark huts
sit round dim lights with Babalawo
throwing their souls in four cowries
on sand, trying to see tomorrow.

Still they pray, the Aladuras pray
to what only hearts can see behind
the curling waves and the sea, the stars
and the subduing unanimity of the sky
and their white bones beneath the sand.

And standing dead on dead sands,
I felt my knees touch living sand—
but the rushing wind killed the budding words.

Dennis Osadebay

## YOUNG AFRICA'S PLEA

Don't preserve my customs
As some fine curios
To suit some white historian's tastes
There's nothing artificial
That bears the natural way,
In culture and ideals of life.
Let me play with the white man's ways.
Let me work with the black man's brains.
Let my affairs sort themselves out.
Then in sweet re-birth
I'll rise a better man,
Not ashamed to face the world.
Those who doubt my talents
In secret fear my strength;
They know I am no less a man.
Let them bury their prejudice,
Let them show their noble sides,
Let me have untrammelled growth.
My friends will never know regret
And I, I never once forget.

Niyi Osundare

## EYEKAIRE

Great Mother of the Earth
White goddess of Osun,
We are here today
From Fields numerous as hair-roots
But hearts glued into one
By adoration.


We team here with issues
Who last year begged for children
You manured the parched land
You strengthened the sower's hand
The tiny gates of earth opened
And seeds sprouted in myriads,
  Mulch their heaps, O Mother,
  And let them grow and fruit
  On roots sturdy like iroko.


We surge in, farmers of the land,
To perform to your mighty drums
Our dance of thanks
Your potent rains transformed
Sand into loam
Heaps' bowels were cushioned,
Tendrils thick as forest-undergrowths
Fed yams huge like rock.
Our barns now rock with yams,
Who once fed on plantains.

Physician Mother,
We trooped here last year
with sores and aches,
Going back home with pots of water
To drink and bath.
Now here in mind and body sound,
We dance various steps to your drums
Without fear of cramps.
Forever shall we live on
The cold cure of your mystery water.


Mother of Plenty,
Mother of Mercy,
Accept these gifts
Conveyed here by the chaste heads
Of seven virgins.
These kolanuts between your meals,
White pigeons to grace your bank,
These yams for you.
Being products of your loam,
This white cloth for you
To clothe your spotless body,
And this parrot feather
To stand aloft on your lofty hair.

Give us health, give us strength,
Splash upon us your water of increase,
The ant-hill never lacks a throng of dwellers.


*Eyekaire means 'the mother we pet.' She is a
woman deified for her good deeds. The immaculate
goddess of fertility and increase. She emanates from
water.*

# A WIFE'S COMPLAINT

Since she came
Things have not been same again
Since this erring chick
Drew in its maggotty trail
The whole house has been
Reeking with garbage-stench
Assaulting every nose,
Pressing us all on nail-edge.

I talk to my husband
He hardly answers
What used to be mine
Is now ours.
My soup tastes stale
Because my spoon is rusty
I am no longer a fitting partner:
The lower edge of a
Wrapper reaching my ankle
Is not smart enough

To show the lower fringes of my buttocks,
This voluminous 'buba' is not low enough
To display the foreridges of my bust.
My legs are too elephantine
For the fast frenzy of today's drums.

It is two-score days now
Since last I stepped the threshold
Of his bedchamber.
Fleeced of my warm sheets,
I must tarry here in harmattan
Expecting the Sun.

This strong gale has shattered
A hut of many years
This new broom has swept
All the golden relics away.

But all this will end,
It must come to a certain sudden end
Sometimes, somewhere, somehow.
Her drum has thundered too loud,
It has reached tearing point.
She had climbed her tree
Past the highest leaf
She is at the brink of a fell fall.

Theirs is now the harmony of wine and water
I shall add a little oil
I bless them with all
That is between cat and mouse,
Between hunter and game;
With the plight of walnuts
Which inhabiting one pod.
Yet forge roomlets of separation.

Mabel Imoukhuede Segun

## THE PIGEON-HOLE

How I wish I could pigeon-hole myself
and neatly fix a label on!
But self-knowledge comes too late
and by the time I've known myself
I am no longer what I was.

I knew a woman once
who had a delinquent child.
She never had a moment's peace of mind
waiting in constant fear,
listening for the dreaded knock
and the cold tones of a policeman:
'Madam, you're wanted at the station.'
I don't know if the knock ever came
but she feared on right until
we moved away from the street.
She used to say,
'It's the uncertainty that worries me—
if only I knew for certain. . .'

If only I knew for certain
what my delinquent self would do. . .
But I never know
until the deed is done
and I live on fearing,
wondering which part of me will be supreme—
the old and tested one, the present
or the future unknown.
Sometimes all three have equal power
and then
I long for a pigeon-hole.

Wole Soyinka

# I THINK IT RAINS

I think it rains
That tongues may loosen from the parch
Uncleave roof-tops of the mouth, hang
Heavy with knowledge.

I saw it raise
The sudden cloud, from ashes.  Settling
They joined in a ring of grey; within
The circling spirit.

O it must rain
These closures on the mind, binding us
In strange despairs, teaching
Purity of sadness.

And how it beats
Skeined transparencies on wings
Of our desires, searing dark longings
In cruel baptisms.

Rain-reeds, practiced in
The grace of yielding, yet unbending
From afar, this, your conjugation with my earth
Bares crouching rocks.


# TELEPHONE CONVERSATION

The price seemed reasonable, location
Indifferent.  The landlady swore she lived
Off premises.  Nothing remained
But self-confession.  'Madam,' I warned,
'I hate a wasted journey — I am African.'

Silence.  Silenced transmission of
Pressurized good-breeding.  Voice, when it came,
Lipstick coated, long gold-rolled
Cigarette-holder pipped.  Caught I was, foully.
'HOW DARK?' . . . I had not misheard. . . .'ARE YOU
    LIGHT
OR VERY DARK?' Button B. Button A. Stench
Of rancid breath of public hide-and-speak.
Red booth.  Red pillar-box.  Red double-tiered
Omnibus squelching tar.  It *was* real!  Shamed
By ill-mannered silence, surrender
Pushed dumbfoundment to beg simplification.
Considerate she was, varying the emphasis —
'ARE YOU DARK? OR VERY LIGHT?'  Revelation came.
'You mean — like plain or milk chocolate?'
Her assent was clinical, crushing in its light
Impersonality.  Rapidly, wave-length adjusted,
I chose.  'West African sepia' — and as afterthought,
'Down in my passport.'  Silence for spectroscopic
Flight of fancy, till truthfulness changed her accent
Hard on the mouthpiece.  'WHAT'S THAT?' conceding
DON'T KNOW WHAT THAT IS.  Like brunette.
'THAT'S DARK, ISN'T IT?'  'Not altogether.
Facially, I am brunette, but madam, you should see
The rest of me.  Palm of my hand, soles of my feet
Are a peroxide blonde.  Friction, caused —
Foolishly madam — by sitting down, has turned
My bottom raven black — One moment madam!' — sensing
Her receiver rearing on the thunderclap
About my ears — 'Madam,' I pleaded, 'wouldn't you
    rather
See for yourself?'

Ken Tsaro-Wiwa

## VOICES

They speak of taxes
Of oil and power

They speak of honour
And pride of tribe

They speak of war
Of bows and arrows

They speak of tanks
And putrid human flesh

I sing my love
For Maria.

Kalu Uka

## FEAR

Last night I heard — it was not in a dream —
the sound of hollow drums and harsh trumpets
as if a village was marching to a graveyard,
last night, when I pasted my ear to the wind
and tasted the spice of eternity on my lips
I had really turned my mind away into fear.

The night grew colder and colder beneath
the blankets and I knew love is always
a thing of wounds, of hurts and smarts,
but fear my countrymen do not understand.
and so in the sound of hollow drums and harsh flutes
we trudge on through silence to eternity.

Only the thunder will revive the drums and flutes
We travellers love so much when they arrive
to warn us, when they whirl from behind
that beautiful shining orphan mountain.

Oh, do not mind this song of flutes and drums
think only of the little stars strung round cradles
think only of the light whose crest we must reach
in the blind rage of the spark divine, think of it,
and night sounds shall be only the anger chained
within our breasts, dark like the deep grave
where souls are pasted to eternity and know not fear!

EARTH TO EARTH (to G.)

As if men hung here unblown,
Their mildewed buds of love like pollen
Late caught, damp in a swollen
Drop of rain; or, like the hot
Tear that chills a fevered pit
After heads into bodies are suckt

Like urine into parched earth
Or ancestral wine into scorched hearth,
And wear ashes and shrivelled petals,

Comes this season of the cassia flower,
And pent passion peers through the bower;
Comes this season, and all labour is fallen
All earthen pitcher as china broken.

Wooing was our labour then,
A trouble-wrapped chrysalis
Grown in the pause taken
Between that visit and this.

The ripest moment is saddest encounter
Performed without banter
In memory of other seasons
Of a lived love now still.

We let this one die;
We let cobwebs sweep
A skein over her face —

On a morning, dewdrops
Are tossed, earth to earth,
Like a veil and a shroud
Over ground imprinted by wooing feet.

Mamman J. Vatsa

## EAGLES

If eagles were to revolt
And form a government
Of their own
They would rule
This our eagle world.
Every strength seeking nation
Has them as a symbol
Of their anticipated strength.

## PRAYERS OF THE COMMONWEALTH

Let our wealth
Be common when none
Is in a state of coma.
If they cut off your oil
Let it remain your toil.
If you're caught in a civil war
May the richer side get the support
Of those member nations
In need of her raw materials.
When in Britain be the guest
Of Enoch Powell
When in Africa be the guest
Of Idi Amin.
Let our wealths
Alter (or do I mean Not) our wealths.

## AN AFRICAN SPECTATOR AT A COMMUNITY
## PROJECT COMMISSIONING IN A EUROPEAN TOWN

In my country
For every official commissioning
Of any community project
We have traditional dances
And spirited libations
Are offered to the gods
And the departed ancestors.
What do you do here?
Everybody is sitting quietly.
No music, no dances
Are your gods annoyed
Or are you annoyed with the gods.
What are you going to tell the ancestors
When they knock at your doors at night
To ask for their offerings?

Okogbule Wonodi

## IROKO

I    Old chronicler
landscape mirror without a memory
whose annals are the cipher
      of blood and earth
      tangled in your veins
seeing and waiting and saying nothing
silent as the desert sand —
who can discover the secrets of the iroko
        on the village square ?

See here
shortlegged generation
striding from peak to peak
      past present
      from past to future
stand a moment and contemplate the iroko
apotheosis of the tense present
waiting
waiting for its date with the bulldozer

II    Come, labyrinth
knowledge makes us unhappy
the iroko tells us nothing

*Sierra Leone*
Syl Cheney Coker

# VOLCANO

*First the innocent*
*next the guilty ones*
*next the makers of occult*
*then my brothers all demons*
*burnt in the fire-dance*
*beat out with gongs*
*on the conga-drum of my back!*

And now this disquisition my Sierra!

was I a part of it
this gust of lava my pox
sordidly oozing into my skull
or Vesuvius madly phallic with rage
crippling the loins of men
somnolent and debauched

afterwards to sweeten their cannibal ecstasy
the lamias in their beds
voluptuous varanuses
insidiously slit open their aortas
thereby betraying their souls
O pedro O mountain
their disgusting appendages

thus seeing this pus at the mouth of a stream
brimming with their foam a stream like a prismatic bird
which at the long eclipse of the sun showed the world
that satyr teaming up with my voyagers
to rape the Sierra Leonean earth
I would drink the sap despoiling my blood

therefore I am raving and ranting
my rotten nose clogging up
my claws piercing my head
I no longer have a country centrifugal and proud
to assuage my long, miserable perdition
also the love which bludgeoned me
afflicted my head like a brain haemorrhage

and now the whirlwind night
lashing my grief right and left
my head at the flash of a whip spins on its neck
obeying the wind in its red madness
awkwardly following the path
my Portuguese conqueror
to you my phantom of steel I say to you

brand me deeper to nourish my bleeding heart!


## CONCERTO FOR AN EXILE

*And the guns roared on*
*in Sierra Leone and Argentina*
*to plunder the tree of agony*
*in my soul!*

The news of the coups the bullets in my soul!
I plunge into the streets holding the dead in my head
I deface my face with my leprous hands
I flee from a pack of hounds
tuned to the reverberations in my heart

what poem shall I write for my fratricidal brothers
whose lust has made the Sierra a volcano too bloody in my life
Brigadier Bangura General La Nusse my soul executioners
what revolutions shall I start for you
they who should join the revolution are dead decalcified body and
     soul
and I am stripped of my vanity my love my joy
my vanity for wishing to marry two continents in love
I know neither the days nor the nights of my days
the nights which cheat me standing headstrong upon my passion

away in Sierra Leone the boulevards of corpses
they shot them and slit their bellies for proof of their subversion
they were men of my salvation so they said who faced the eunuch
     Christ
lying upside down on that ravaged Sierra Leonean earth
and drunkenly talked about Che writing illogicalities for revolts
but in speaking of those revolutions a savage bird entered my soul
to sing me a concerto for pain my lady sang me a concerto of
     betrayal
that senorita's sex too sweet too vicious to my soul!

and I come to you once again Pedro da Cinta
my Portuguese conquistador my Sierra my volcano
was I a part of it the eruption tearing my country apart
I have my Nova Scotian madness my tree of agony
and let my brothers know I walk the streets of exile
clutching their bullets in my soul!

Crispin George

# WEIGH YOUR WORDS

Simple words may wound or soothen,
Much depending on their use;
They estrange as well as sadden
When their use becomes abuse.

Air may be compared to verbiage
Both in quality and mass;
Furious air will scatter foliage
Thoughtless words good friends disperse.

Temperate words tend to ennoble,
Comfort, quicken, and console,
When, like viands on the table
They revive the hungry soul.

Words, like atom-bombs, are heinous,
When they hurt both friend and foe;
Dangerous, cowardly and callous,
These are harbingers of woe.

Words may light the fuse of carnage,
They may strike the oil of peace;
Be you cautious how you manage,
That your words go not amiss.

Weigh them in the scales of justice
And be sure of their control;
Do not wing your words at random,
They may fly beyond their goal.

Words are justly termed immortal,
Whether spoken or engraved;
Therefore tarry at the portal
Till their passage-way be paved.

Delphine King

## THE CHILD

When will this child be black?
When will the child in ebony be carved
Who occupies a place conspicuous there
Where all our guests arrive?
Who greets them first?  A child!
A child that calmly pours
Out of a bowl into the fountain pure
The flowing liquid;
But behold the child is white.

The image of conditioned minds
Unwitting, unsuspectingly exposed
In the figure of a child
To all the world who look to us
For inspiration, leadership.
When will the child in ebony carved,
When will the child be black?

# THE MEANING OF AFRICA

Africa, you were once just a name to me
But now you lie before me with sombre green challenge
To that loud faith for freedom (life more abundant)
Which we once professed shouting
Into the silent listening microphone
Or on an alien platform to a sea
Of white perplexed faces troubled
With secret Imperial guilt; shouting
Of you with a vision euphemistic
As you always appear
To your lonely sons on distant shores.


Then the cold sky and continent would disappear
In a grey mental mist.
And in its stead the hibiscus blooms in shameless scarlet
and the bougainvillea in mauve passion
entwines itself around strong branches;
the palm trees stand like tall proud moral women
shaking their plaited locks against the
cool suggestive evening breeze;
the short twilight passes;
the white full moon turns its round gladness
towards the swept open space
between the trees; there will be
dancing tonight; and in my brimming heart
plenty of love and laughter.
Oh, I got tired of the cold Northern sun
Of white anxious ghost-like faces
Of crouching over heatless fires
In my lonely bedroom.

The only thing I never tired of
Was the persistent kindness
Of you too few unafraid
Of my grave dusky strangeness.


So I came back
Sailing down the Guinea Coast.
Loving the sophistication
Of your brave new cities:
Dakar, Accra, Cotonou,
Lagos, Bathurst and Bissau;
Liberia, Freetown, Libreville,
Freedom is really in the mind.


Go up-country, so they said,
To see the real Africa.
For whomsoever you may be,
That is where you come from.
Go for bush, inside the bush,
You will find your hidden heart.
Your mute ancestral spirit.
And so I went, dancing on my way.


Now you lie before me passive
With your unanswering green challenge.
Is this all you are?
This long uneven red road, this occasional succession
Of huddled heaps of four mud walls
And thatched, falling grass roofs
Sometimes ennobled by a thin layer
Of white plaster, and covered with thin
Slanting corrugated zinc.
These patient faces on weather-beaten bodies

Bowing under heavy market loads.
The pedalling cyclist wavers by
On the wrong side of the road,
As if uncertain of this new emancipation.
The squawking chickens, the pregnant she-goats
Lumber awkwardly with fear across the road.
Across the windscreen view of my four-cylinder kit car
An overladen lorry speeds madly towards me
Full of produce, passengers, with driver leaning
Out into the swirling dust to pilot his
Swinging obsessed vehicle along.

Beside him on the raised seat his first-class
Passenger clutching and timid; but he drives on
At so, so many miles per hour, peering out with
Bloodshot eyes, unshaved face and dedicated look;
His motto painted on each side: *Sunshine Transport,*
*We get you there quick, quick. The Lord is my Shepherd.*

The red dust settles down on the green leaves.

I know you will not make me want, Lord,
Though I have reddened your green pastures
It is only because I have wanted so much
That I have always been found wanting.
From South and East, and from my West
The sandy desert holds the North.
We look across a vast Continent
And blindly call it ours.
You are not a Country, Africa,
You are a concept,
Fashioned in our minds, each to each,
To hide our separate fears,
To dream our separate dreams.
Only those within you who know

Their circumscribed Plot,
And till it well with steady plough
Can from that harvest then look up
To the vast blue inside
Of the enamelled bowl of sky
Which covers you and say
"This is my Africa" meaning
"I am content and happy.
I am fulfilled, within,
Without and roundabout.
I have gained the little longings
Of my hands, my loins, my heart,
And the soul following in my shadow."
I know now that is what you are Africa:
Happiness, contentment, and fulfillment,
And a small bird singing on a mango tree.

## NIGHTSONG CITY

Sleep well, my love, sleep well:
the harbour lights glaze over restless docks,
police cars cockroach through the tunnel streets;

from the shanties creaking iron-sheets
violence like a bug-infested rag is tossed
and fear is immanent as sound in the wind-swung bell;

the long day's anger pants from sand and rocks;
but for this breathing night at least,
my land, my love, sleep well.

The sounds begin again:
the siren in the night
the thunder at the door
the shriek of nerves in pain.

Then the keening crescendo
of faces split by pain
the wordless, endless wail
only the unfree know.

Importunate as rain
the wraiths exhale their woe
over the sirens, knuckles, boots;
my sounds begin again.

from POEM


Somehow we survive
and tenderness, frustrated, does not wither.

Investigating searchlights rake
our naked unprotected contours;

. . . . . . . . .

boots club on the peeling door.

But somehow we survive
severance, deprivation, loss.

Patrols uncoil along the asphalt dark
hissing their menace to our lives,

most cruel, all our land is scarred with terror,
rendered unlovely and unlovable;
sundered are we and all our passionate surrender

but somehow tenderness survives.

Zweli Ed Dladla

## EPITAPH ON FACES

I cannot remember you my brother.
Perhaps it is the snow in your eyes.
Let me wipe the cold in your death-eyes . . .
or your lips are sordid from the penny-songs you seem to sing.

I cannot hear your voice.
It shines beyond the cackle of queen jezebel who fed the peasants
with caviar and pumpkin-seeds when they discovered the corn
stuffed in her bloomers under her pillow.

"Twas a noble gesture" remarked the albino who counted dimes
under his tongue while winking at the sun.

For a while I thought I knew you my brother.
Let's chant mayibuye/comeback together thus walking back to
the future we forgot.
Or, is your voice brassed by the golden handles of your coffin?

Perhaps I can reach you from below here.
Kings are buried in/with their knapsacks you know.
Will that hinder your hand from holding mine?

I cannot remember you my brother.
Kaffirboy and niggerboy are dying too.
Will that sound too sad for you?

I was told at the morgue it was about time.
But somehow I have suspicions they are masquerading as you.
What a lonesome death they should die in souls and bodies
not their own.
Or perhaps I didn't know you my brother.

The streets and the shanties were your camouflage.
But I cannot believe in reincarnation if the fuhrer and voster
are to come as du pont merged in your body.
But again my mind is burned to ashen butterflies.
Let me remember you my brother not in the bondage we all
   shunned.

## II.

Resurrection is no jew monopoly/or juju for those to die.

I can hear you still.
Your fury shrill in the melody of your penny-whistle,
shrieking beautiful obscenities in the corners of eloff
to the delight of your unlistening audience who toss dimes
and pennies at your feet while you wail and sing, niggerboy
niggerboy, kaffirboy kaffirboy, till when?

## ELEGY FOR MY CONTEMPORARIES

Bones on a telegraph-pole
Dance their epitaph
To those born rich and healthy,

Young men, clean-limbed, clear-eyed,
Those who wore the clothes
Of dying children.

They were not without love
Or beauty; their hands were tied
To the wheels of brilliance

And they whirled like gunfire
In the night. I name them
Among my friends, my people,

Those who married well, who loved
Their children, who gave
What their pockets allowed.

They shall die in their doorways
And in the streets, thrombosis
And murder pay their debts—

You cannot count them now, the lines
Of soldiers who drank deeply
From the jewelled cup of safety.

Timothy Holmes

## THE CONQUERED

Refuged in secret places far from concourses,
Hidden near living rock, home among windiness,
A long breath self-promised into the future,
Peril came to our valley, shirring flat waters
With smoke, dust of ironstone, startling soft palates.

Viewing land fastnesses, western protectors,
Seeing on bronzed hill-curves filtered sunlight,
Our evening blaze a comfort, air-sweetener,
With a rush of starlings night was present:
On those distant clifftops, a line of fires lighted
Their smoke, a burnt bitter, towards us blown.

From both sides advancing portents of danger,
Choking encroachment, forewarnings confirmed,
Broad lanes to a future closed up with poisons.
Walls of our refuge draw us against them.
Pressed us right through them, hid us behind,
Leaving small shadows of us and our chattels
Painted upon them. For others.

## REACTION TO CONQUEST

Three blows from a steel axe
Broke through the heart
Of a rare, extinction-threatened tree
Which though standing yet
Browns to fall.

Such was the time of year
That tight-skinned berries,
Waiting to explode, dried too soon,
And clatter-clattered
To the ground.

Around the root-tops, naked once
Hungry grass has crept
Now moss, bark-feeding insects,
Woodpeckers, fungus,
Dark leaf-mould.

Keropatse Kgositsile

## MY PEOPLE NO LONGER SING

Remember
 When my echo upsets
 The plastic windows of your mind
 And darkness invades its artificial light
 The pieces of your regrets hard to find
         Remember
 I shall only be a sighing memory then
 Until you look in the fiery womb of sunrise
 Retrieving songs almost aborted
 On once battered black lips
Remember
 When you get sickandtired
 of being sick and tired
 To remind the living
 That the dead cannot remember.

## YES MANDELA. . .

Yes, Mandela, we shall be moved
We are Men enough to have a conscience
We are Men enough to immortalize your song
We are Men enough to look Truth straight in the face

To defy the devils who traded in the human Spirit

For Black cargoes and material superprofits
We emerge to sing a Song of Fire with Roland

We emerge to prove Truth cannot be enslaved
In chains or imprisoned in an island inferno
We emerge to stand Truth on her two feet We emerge

To carry the banner of humanism across the face of the Earth

Our voice in unison with our poet's proudly says
'Change is gonna come!'

Bloke Modisane

## LONELY

it gets awfully lonely,
lonely;
like screaming,
screaming lonely;
screaming down dream alley,
screaming of blues, like none can hear;
but you hear me clear and loud:
echoing loud;
like it's for you I scream.

I talk to myself when I write,
shout and scream to myself,
then to myself
scream and shout:
shouting a prayer,
screaming noises,
knowing this way I tell
the world about still lives;
even maybe
just to scream and shout.

is it I lack the musician's contact
direct?
or, is it true, the writer
creates
(except the trinity with God, the machine and he)

incestuous silhouettes
to each other scream and shout,
to me shout and scream
pry and mate;
inbred deformities of loneliness.

Ezekiel Mphahlele

## VIGNETTES

### I

The thing we are talking about tonight
is part of the great fight we are carrying on
and it represents a forward and an upward look —
a pushing onward. You and I have been breasting
hills; we have been climbing upward; there
has been progress and we can see it day by day
looking back along blood-filled paths. . . .

W.E.B. Du Bois, *The Crisis*, Oct. 1926

I wonder why those geese
keep haunting me
daring me, it seems, to
make this poem.
I saw them
breasting the wind
across the slopes of greenery
one morning.
Stopped in my jogging tracks
and counted
I'd say at least
three score of them.

you and I have been breasting hills. . . .

They flaunted patterns
of brown and black
and roan and white
and green,
walking on the slope
as if ahead

were bearers of a coffin,
or they were pickets
bent on raising hell for
bureaucrats
and telling them their goose was cooked
and they must deliver —
a purpose much bigger
than the crumbs of bread
these numskulls
come and throw to them
over the fence.

you and I have been breasting hills. . . .

Then it was I learned
                again
as I had done so many times
                that
nature can be mean or kind
                and elegant
for no other reason
than the dumb urge
to move from here
                to there.
I could myself
have been a goose
walking on a slope of greenery
drawn by the mute
togetherness and chaos of life:

haven't you and I been breasting hills? . . . .

Then one night I dreamed
those geese were raising cackling hell
at the garment factory:
WE WANT MORE PAY AND BENEFITS!

Then the tanks came out and blew
the geese
                  to feathereens,
insides flying all over the place. . . .

<u>you and I have been breasting hills</u>. . . .


Next day I went
once more
to the pond by the hill.
The geese were scattered
on the hillside
doing different things and nothings:
yes, so much for dreams!


I wonder why those geese
keep haunting me
daring me, it seems, to
make this poem.
Now it seems that
                  beauty
will not last for its own sake.
Beauty only means the
                  parts are put together right
                  to shape the order that you want.


And when I see it,
'tseems it can't be true
could <u>be</u> such order
as a flock of geese
walking across a hill of greenery
serene and breasting the wind.
And so the tanks of fire. . . .
and up the thing will go in feathers!

You see,
they poisoned beauty for me
at the very source
in the painful south
except what we could salvage
from the tyranny of time and place
for ourselves and others:
and of course ——

you and I have been breasting hills. . . .


## 2

I see this prof
stomping up 34th
breasting the wind
and make a broadside
down Chestnutt,
mackintosh billowing behind him,
afro head thrown forward,
mouth open slightly,
and he stomps as if
to measure his father's land
and peg a claim.

I say to myself:
that prof has pantzer divisions
in his head,
                blueprints
of some deadly business
                in his bag
and somebody'll have
                to beware:
I know this because
                you and I have been breasting hills. . . .

3

I see this dude —
six feet of elegance
        and style —
take his time
        down 34th:
capacious hat
throws
        a shade of subtle menace
over
        his quick-moving eyes:
a long grey coat
        with fringe of fur top and bottom
he casts
        a figure so delicate
the wind might break him.
But I watch him
        scrape the wind
with left hand
        like he's steering
body through a fissure in the wind,
        while weaving
bending away
        from its cutting edge.
The wind keeps coming on
        but he's breasting it:
been coming on long's
        he can remember.
No pantzer divisions
        in his head
no bag no blueprints:
        knows the art
                of feeling good and bad,
                        of dying many times,
cutting corners cutting losses —

victories are so little
you must hug them
        feel them:
to pay your debts you've got forever.
And while he preens himself
        before the sidewalk window
they're on top of him —
        the minions of the law —
bung him into the car,
but not before he turns
        to look at me:
What do I see
        in that face but the
                landscape where
poetry and history
        make their concourse.
And I, sitting here tonight,
what do I know
                but that
the geese made fat by all the folks
who love only things that cannot talk —
those geese can only die
                in my poisoned dream;
                but that
the dude will live a people's poetry,
                their history;
                but that
the prof must go on stomping into
                fortresses
to stake our claim
and even sometimes beat them
                at their game
in the night of stratagems
in the open daylight of debate?
What do I know, I say,

                    but that
you and I are always breasting hills?
Otherwise
                    this poem must die and you the gods
will have to tell me something else tonight.

                                4

Bra Moremi
comes up Newtown Street
heading for downtown Jo'burg,
swinging shoulder,
hands in pockets,
like litter in the streets
the reek of factory pork
and gingerbearded winos
could never touch him.


you and I have been breasting hills. . . . .

never mind:
                    ta-night is ta-night Missus Rosenbaum.
Katusi sends his brothers off to school
                    this morning,
Pa and Ma have gone to white man's town. . . . .
                    ta-night is ta-night Missus Rosenbaum,
ta-night your jewels are mine.

Down Eloff Street
            he pushes through
the multi-colored crowd
like there wasn't
            pinkies around
ready any time to kick
            shove him off
just to feel
            who they are.

94

You see him pushing the south and then you know
he's staying on the line
they set for him —
the way those railway tracks
have pushed aside the bush
and thread their way
between the hills
tapering out in the distance
far's the eye can see,
dominant and lonely.


you and I have been breasting hills. . . . . . .


never mind:
          ta-night is ta-night Missus Rosenbaum.
Vukani's bathing grandpa's feet
          this morning.
Pa has followed Ma into the Night. . . . . .
          ta-night is ta-night Missus Rosenbaum,
ta-night your jewels are mine.


Yesterday
          our fathers shook the earth
beneath their shoeless feet,
breasting hills and winds;
their song and shout
          flooded valleys,
brought the night tumbling down
          on laagered enemy;
Soon
          only the memory of song and shout and smoke
would hang over the trail
          of blood and debris.

Today
        this juba
has to push through crowds
        on enemy ground —
today
        when heroes are minted
in the braveries of prison islands,
hanging head down from a noose
        in the butcher's cold-cold cells,
done in by cops
        whose teeth were filed in their mother's womb;
today,
        when parliament is full of
rabid cats and hooded ghouls
and barricades itself with hounds and guns,
        out of reach
for messengers or plumbers, clerks or profs
        who only stomp and push their blackness
far as you can spit.


you and I have been breasting hills. . . . . .


never mind:
        ta-night is ta-night Missus Rosenbaum.
He swore he'd never leave his big-eyed woman
        yesterday night
For Pa and Ma they went their separate ways. . . .
        ta-night is ta-night Missus Rosenbaum,
ta-night your jewels are mine.


For three young men —
Moremi and Vukani and Katusi —
history began when they were born;
but their blood,
        their fathers' earth,

will always ring
                the Elders' song of bygone days that
— come renewal time —
                will sew together all the scattered epics
of our day.

He said for them to meet at Clarendon Circle . . . . get it
together, Vukani! . . . bring the Rosenbaum pick-up after
pork deliveries . . . go on to Clarendon . . . . Katusi'll
bring the tools, remember Clarendon Circle now . . . when
the clock strikes ten at the Greek man's corner . . . we
move we move to Rosenbaum . . . . we'll take him one of his
pork sausages. . . . . .

For now
                no elegance of geese
                no style of cadillac brothers
                there across the seas;
but don't they say that you and I and all
                from east to west
have all the years been breasting hills and winds
                the size of a whole black universe? — — —

never mind:
                for ta-night is ta-night Missus Rosenbaum,
ta-night your jewels are mine.

C. D. Noble

# WHO IS THE RAIN?

DEDICATION:  To Dan


Didn't it rain? Well, didn't it?
The night of the 18th,
Didn't it hail
Saturday?
Yeah!  it stormed January
Yep!  in Jeppestown
Coming twa, twa, twang
bullets slumping walls
down in that sloot where
my mother used to play
barefooted when she was growing up in
    Main Street
and
ricochetted
        weight and crush of hailstones
        damned
        Concrete'll have to swim
        Granite to float
        Iron and steel to tread
        water
    warily
We're welling up
                we're water and ice
freezing fire the heat could not thaw
                we're the poor
clashing with modern motors
crashing plate-glassed pioneers obscure
behind a uniform, armed,
standing guard
against the frosted dark

Look!
　　　with pangas and choppers
　　　how the children play
　　　in townships now
　　　targets for guns
　　　tasting slaughter for blood
from our rain-goddesses
testing patient suffering
who best can bear
the acts ,of God
levelling off
massed clouds barricaded
we lean on this collapsed
　　　city shrinking our black urban culture
　　　cleaned up
　　　for pumped-up consumption at the Brooke
　　　where earning bread Ipi-Tombi
　　　actresses and actors
play

What play is this?
　　　we can't go, outcast, barred
　　　　　　　　　　black
　　　　　　　　　　the skies
　　　　　　　　　　the dams are bursting

We're drops of life
the tense surface
drowning death
built new in
reeking vile
septic houses and plagued pipes
floating sewage
retching the offal of
long years we've fed on
disease we're used to

We're living waters, immune,
springing from sources, like history, like heaven,
that cannot be banned,
exiled,
or courted:

"When it rains, it rains"
        and fine ladies'll take off more than shoes
in the tidal forceful time

                                rouge, powder and
                                lipstick,
                                mascara too
the complete cosmetic
facade
before
graced in new identities
we'll smile
one week-working day, brightly
and greet, convention-like, discovered
Brothers and Sisters saying
"Well, didn't it rain, didn't it?"

Oswald Mtshali

## AMAGODUKA AT GLENCOE STATION

We travelled a long journey
Through the wattle forests of Vryheid,
cross the low-levelled Blood River
whose water flowed languidly
as if dispirited for the
shattered glory of my ancestors.

We passed the coalfields of Dundee—
blackheads in the wrinkled face
of Northern Zululand—
until our train ultimately came
to a hissing stop at Glencoe.

Many people got off
leaving the enraged train
to snort and charge at the night
on it's way to Durban.

The time was 8 p.m.

I picked up my suitcase,
sagging under the weight of a heavy overcoat
I shambled to the "non-European Males" waiting room.

The room was crowded
the air hung, a pall of choking odour,
rotten meat, tobacco and sour beer.

Windows were shut tight
against the sharp bite of winter.

Amagoduka sat on bare floor
their faces sucking the warmth
of the coal fire crackling in the corner.

They chewed dried bread
scooped corned beef with rusty knives,
and drank *mgombothi* from the plastic can
which they passed from mouth to mouth.

They spoke animatedly
and laughed in thunderous peals.

A girl peeped through the door,
they shuddered at the sudden cold blast,
jumped up to fondle and leer at her
"*Hau! ngena Sisi!* — Oh! come in sister!"

She shied like a frightened filly
banged the door and bolted.
They broke into tumultuous laughter.

One of them picked up a guitar
plucked it with broken finger nails
caressed its strings with a castor oil bottle—
it sighed like a jilted girl.
"You play down! Phansi! Play D" he whispered.

Another joined in with a concertina,
its sound fluttered in flowery notes
like a butterfly picking pollen from flower to flower.

The two began to sing,
their voices crying for the mountains
and the hills of Msinga, stripped naked of
their green garment.

They crossed rivers and streams,
gouged dry by the sun rays,
where lowing cattle genuflected

for a blade of grass and a drop of water
on riverbeds littered with carcasses and bones.

They spoke of hollow-cheeked maidens
heaving drums of brackish water
from a far away fountain.

They told of big-bellied babies
sucking festering fingers
instead of their mothers shrivelled breasts.

Two cockroaches
as big as my overcoat buttons
jived across the floor
snatched meat and bread crumbs
and scurried back to their hideout.

The whole group joined in unison:
curious eyes peered through frosted windows
*"Ekhaya bafowethu!*—Home brothers!"

We come from across the Tugela river,
we are going to eGoli! eGoli! eGoli!
where they'll turn us into moles
that eat the gold dust
and spit out blood.

Arthur Nortje

## WAITING

The isolation of exile is a gutted
warehouse at the back of pleasure streets:
the waterfront of limbo stretches panoramically—
night the beautifier lets the lights
dance across the wharf.
I peer through the skulls black windows
wondering what can credibly save me.
The poem trails across a ruined wall
a solitary snail, or phosphorescently
swims into vision like a fish
through a hole in the mind's foundation, acute
as a glittering nerve.

Origins trouble the voyager much, those roots
that have sipped the waters of another continent.
Africa is gigantic, one cannot begin
to know even the strangest behaviour furthest
south in my xenophobic department.
Come back, come back mayibuye
cried the breakers of stone and cried the crowds
cried Mr. Kumalo before the withering fire
mayibuye Afrika.

Now there is loneliness of lost
beauties at Cabo de Esperancia, Table Mountain:
all the dead poets who sang of spring's
miraculous recrudescence in the sandscapes of Karoo
sang of thoughts that pierced like arrows, spoke
through the strangled threat of multi-humanity
bruised like a python in the maggot-fattening sun.

You with your face of pain, your touch of gaiety,
with your eyes that could distil me any instant
have passed into some diary, some dead journal
now that the computer, the mechanical notion
obliterates sincerities.
The amplitude of sentiment has brought me no nearer
to anything affectionate,
new magnitude of thought has but betrayed
the lustre of your eyes.

You yourself have vacated the violent arena
for a northern life of semi-snow
under the Distant Early Warning System:
I suffer the radiation burns of silence.
It is not cosmic immensity or catastrophe
that terrifies me:
it is solitude that mutilates,
the night bulb that reveals ash on my sleeve.

# WINDSCAPE

Air-swept slopes of straining weed
plunge dimly to the dung-dry rocks,
shore cowers under the bilious sky.
The oil-scummed green sea heaves and slides
below my view from concrete heights
in struggle with the lurching wind,
Chopping into the curve the white surge
sprawls among beats in frothing nipples.

Sharp winds with venom flay
the brittle bones
or tug in ferocious gusts at clothes:
Rex Trueform suit from a summer shop
(what man about town, distinctive style?).
Around my limbs the wool rags bloat.

Into the lull with movement treason
I stride braced with a rod, resistance sweet,
The Lash bites back, a plane of grit
sheers up, obliquely. Note
how eyes squint hard into destiny's balance.

Hug
walls and walk flat and
anticipate but don't look back
or spit in the sun's pale skimming face.

The street funnels flotsam; air floats, deceptive;
black wires dirge, then, take this door.
The wild slut howls for rain
to soothe her caked and aching hollows.

Sydney Sipho Sepamla

## SILENCE

The silence I speak of
stretches the moment to Pretoria
Bioemfontein and Cape Town
it is the same silence
that has walled in
tense remembrances of days
making'of each moment
pebbles of time

the silence I speak of
tends to confound my tongue
I gurgle speech sounds
like a river sipping
the marrow of aged rocks

the silence I speak of
crouches the night
to make shadows that terrorise
even the illusions I fabricate

daily I collide with ghosts
that walk day-night streets
hourly I feel the howling of
their wintered hearts
break into the ease
I've learnt to pace

I've sought to read
the brooding silence
that betrays itself with
dry coughs
or unfolding wrinkles

sometimes I've gone down
on all fours
raking the earth with one ear
to pick what murmurs
may glide down there
beneath the roots

how this silence
I hear
breeds
on avenues of despair
I'll never know

I speak
of a silence
I fear.

# PIGEON-HOLES

Now that we walk on Church Street
Straddle double-lanes in Commissioner Street
Frolic up and down Voortrekker Street
Squat on tables at the Union Buildings
Take our place in offices at Parliament
And have our appendicitis removed at Hospital
Let us not forget to heed messages
Passing through pierced ear-lobes
Or fail to sprinkle white salt
On dark embers of a brazier
Let not the anchor of our faith
Be in a few jars of Metamorphosa
Nor lanky tubes of Artra
But let us recall
We were about to tame our scars
About to shout: Freedom Now
But the rattle of a gun
Shook the very roots of our kinky hair
Scattered the fathers of our nests
Like the hellish dust of a 'copter
Now we bridge feelings
With long days of anguish
We try to settle the debt
Sweat dripping in long queues
Because all the pigeon-holes remain.

## DEATH SURVEY

i had a dream
true like i'm black like this
conflict.
a dream fell on my head that sleeps still like a stone
my head on the bed
the stone in the donga
i had a dream last night
it fell like a feather into my sleep.
a friend came running into the yard and his face was like a
                                                    horror
a death running wildly loose
when some guys i know came running after him
charging
like dogs so vicious
barking and chasing a cow from a dustbin
my friend came rushing into my house
i ran
could not keep my eyes off from the sparkling knives
dangling over my shoulders
and bricks flying over my head like this
we ran
i was calling my friend's name
he called mine too
and we could not keep off from that gaping donga
which was swallowing my scream and desperately needed
                                                    my life
why did gatsha come
because there he was holding some meeting with the old leg
                                                    of the past
sitting in a circle.
i saw them take a kerrie and try to beat out some brain
out of a boy who was kneeling and trying to scream

frightened
i ran loose
to frank's place at ninth avenue and found that the bulldozer
had been there
before me
i stumbled over bricks
they bit my toes like hungry rats
and something was in my ear
a cockroach
desperately wanting to hide inside my ear
its long legs frantic
its sharp small head digging right through
cruel
even screams don't come in a dream like this
why
this bloody bulldozer had done a good job and its teeth
dripped blood;
bricks-pillars-hunks-of-concrete-zincs-broken-steps-doors-
broken-glasses-crooked window-panes-broken-flower-
pots-planks-twisted-shoes
lay all over the show
like a complete story,
i ran
my toes bleeding
and i held my heart in my right hand
like a jacket.

# A WISH TO LIE DOWN

The night silence falls lightly on my head
and the dark shadow wraps my heart
but the noise of the barking dogs
and cricket
and the silent sound of silence which seems to be holding the
                                                              future
cracks and snaps my long faded peace
and I sit here
jail starvation and death
seem to want to hold my hand
as lovers do,
Who have long not been together.
I miss what I do not know
for what I know I wish not to have known;
time
like a thief has long robbed me a wish
to lie down, listen and look into the blue
and let my blood like a river,
flow to its destination —
my heart beats like cars flying over a freeway
the mind
buzzes like a whirlwind
and I wish and I want
the dogs crickets and silence itself could lie down and sleep
                                but sleep now fall into me
like night into day
and my friend there, turning and rolling in bed
has his eyes closed and head covered
he is silent
only so he can hear the throb in his head
and perhaps —

fall asleep in the process;
peace
even sleep does not know it
for sleep lately, is a lover of nightmares.


## A POEM ON BLACK AND WHITE


if i pour petrol on a white child's face
and give flames the taste of his flesh
it won't be a new thing
i wonder how i will feel when his eyes pop
and when my nostrils sip the smell of his flesh
and his scream touches my heart
i wonder if i will be able to sleep;
i understand alas i do understand
the rage of a whiteman pouring petrol on a black child's face
setting it alight and shooting him in a pretoria street,
pretoria has never been my home
i have crawled its streets with pain
i have ripped my scrotal sack at every door i intended entering
in that city
and jo'burg city has never seen me, has never heard me
the pain of my heart has been the issue of my heart
sung by me
freezing in the air
but who has not been witness to my smile?
yet, alexandra's night shadow is soaked and drips with my
tears.

## THE DEAD BIRD

Dead on my palm
A slab of silent meat
Suspended between stiffness and rotting
Bones sitting stolid on my skin
The beak clamped tight
Unsoftened by the feathers
A final refusal
Hanging determined from the weak neck
Eyes bright with liquid
Desperate with concentrated feeling
Smouldering into me
The sun's lens-captured heat finding a point to scorch
The curling feathers, screams,
Imprisoning the whole world's silences
Recoiling from my foreign breath
Pink skin drily accepting feather ends
Rustling cage of feathers
Flapping and raging in my mind
Would never float wind-lightened
Empty itself of song
Because a pump refused to beat
An eternity of grace
Cradled and responsive in my hand.

## 14. OASIS

Listen to the sandy tunes
Of the desert song
As it rides the sand dunes
Accompanied by the winds
Singing through the palm leaves,

I want to hold hands
With the Arabs
And dance together
With the Israelis,
We shall dance
By an oasis
And cool our feet and hearts
With the water
Of the oasis!

I want to dance the rumba
and the cha cha cha,
I want to dance the white dances
Of the west
And shuffle my feet
Softly on the polished
And powdered wooden floor,

I want to dance
The dances of yellow men
At sunset . . .
Show me the sword dance
Of the Russians
And I will dance,
I will dance the bamboo
Dance of the Chinese

And the rice dance
Of the Japanese,
I will dance with the
Garlanded Vietnamese girls
In the swamps . . .

You deaf Brother
Standing there with a club
In your hand,
Can you not read
My sign language?

Cut off this rope,
Open the steel gate,
I want to dance the dances
Of colonialists and communists,
I want to try the dances
Of neo-colonialists
And African socialists,
I want to dance the dances
Of our friends and
The dances of our enemies,
I want to lift their daughters
To my shoulder
And elope with them . . .

Let the Eskimo play and sing
His snowy song
And I will dance
To its whaley rhythm,

Let the Spanish girls
Snap their song
With their fingers
And I will dance like a cock
Wooing a hen,

Let the Zulu girls
Click their mountain song
With their sweet tongues
And will join the men,
We will strike the earth
Like the falling meteorite!

Listen to the wailing tune
Of the Indian song,
Listen to the purring drums,
I will touch the earth lightly
Like a butterfly
And twist my limbs
To the piercing rhythm
Of the lyre,

I want to hold
The delicate waist
Of the untouchable goddess
In sari,

I want to touch
The vibrating buttocks
Of the Muganda girl
Dancing the *nankasa,*

Let me strike the beaded navel
of the *dingidingi* dancer . . .
Let me dance
And forget my sorrow,
Let me forget
That I am jobless
And landless,

Forget that I am hopeless
And helpless,
Let me sweat out my frustrations
And anger,

Who wants to know
That his children
Will never go to school
Will never get a job
Or land
Or Cow
Or goat?

Let me dance
And forget!

Rose Mbowa

RUIN

Up on a hill it stood immovable,
Dark and gloomy in the dusk;
A heavy silence hung in the air
Restraining her courage, her will;
But on she walked.

A cricket whistled, breaking the silence,
Lighting her path and her will;
Then suddenly it stopped,
As if suppressed by a heavy hand,
Still . . . on she moved.

Every move drew her nearer,
Every move gravitated towards the gloom;
Giant trees, heavy and dark before her rose,
Guards on duty, erect in the dark,
Through them she pushed.

With eyes closed, arms outstretched,
She groped in an envelope of black;
The air grew dense and doomed,
Her heart drummed faster and louder;
To the floor she stepped.

With trembling hands she pushed,
A squeal pierced the air;
Flashes blinded her sight;
And down she descended at a blow,
On the grim rude stone.

# ASIA

# ASIAN POETS

Some of the poets included here are well known. Quite a few (us) make their home in the West. When a poet reaches excellence, his poems often recapture experiences which are from his own life; some seeking identity within the roots and some in the branches they've sprouted under an alien climate. A poet cannot be separated from his ethnic identity, though the choice of enlarging on it is entirely up to him. Writers leave their homeland for one reason or another and seek a new one. In the early pangs of alienation some may feel they've lost or sacrificed their poetic identity. If the poet perseveres and has faith in his own self he surely overcomes this dilemma as the Asian poets who live in the West and are included in this section have ably shown.

Presumably, the poets in this section grew up in an era in which their "second language", or the language of intellectual upbringing was English. We chose to write in English. A creative writer needs no defense for his choice of linguistic medium nor is any needed no matter what some anthologists might think. The choice of creative expression in a language is self-willed and self-propelled by one's confidence and fecundity in that language. The only relevant criterion is how well one writes in it and is sustained by it. Quite a few of the poets here have established themselves as some of the best poets and novelists by any standard. This by itself speaks eloquently for their success and achievement.

A writer's destiny is not altogether within his control. His "fame" or "obscurity" is controlled by factors I do not wish to go into. However, the burden of establishing an identity has been harder on Asian poets writing in English. We're a minority among minorities. Often a significant work by one of us stands not as representative of the group but as one's own measure of success. America is generous to the Arts but when it comes to minorities, the Asian poet writing in English is yet to find acceptance or collectively establish the value of his heritage. We have to be "exceptional" to be considered "good" and perhaps win the Pulitzer to be considered "exceptional"! Yet such are the rules of being a poet writing in English in the Western world having been born in the East. It may take long for contemporary Asian poets to make themselves felt as an integral part of American letters, and still retain their ethnic identity such as the Jewish, the Black and the American Indian writers have. By and large, American editors of little magazines and journals, and the younger American audience have been most encouraging and sympathetic to our cause as they are to all fair and neglected causes which somehow touch their lives. They've realized the terrible alienation one might particularly create in the Arts if one applied the same "politics" that the rulers of governments often do to eliminate the vital influence of the poet on the conscience of a people.

The reader will find in this small but eclectic selection of poems, a poetry that is strikingly original and reveals a mature understanding of what makes a contemporary poem.


G.S. Sharat Chandra

*Burma*
U Win Pe

A TIME TO TIE THE MIND

Wetness comes to the skies.
Floor-planks in the corner grow mildew.
In the once brown garden
Roses suck the sub-surface water
And tiny shoots tremble the earth with their burgeoning.
This is the time for winning
That which has yet to be won.
Time to place the breath before the mind.
Time to tie the mind to the breath.
This loosening bundle will soon not be worth
The earth it displaces.
The refore should you gladly expend it
For that experience which comprehends all time.

## POEM FOR WAZO

Wetness comes to the skies.
Earth trembles with the thrust of tiny shoots.
At the bottom of the monastery-garden
The rising stream swings to the river
And the sea.  This is the time for winning
That which has yet to be won.
Time to place the breath before the mind,
Time to tie the mind to the breath.
Not to seek for that which is not
On the topless towers of vain speculation,
In ritual's craftshop nor the mirrored
Halls of the self.  There are the worlds
And all of time in the passing
Touch of breath on the lip; to watch this
In the nakedness of phenomenality
Like a candle-flame, and when all is gathered
In immediate singleness
To let it all go, to know.
This loosening bundle will soon not be worth
The earth it displaces.
Therefore should it not be expended
In doing that which has yet to be done.

*India*
G.S. Sharat Chandra

## SECOND JOURNEY

In the gullet fish
the fisherman's touch
becomes art  the needle
the color of breath

It's here the hole is sewn
on bone by women
whose fingers name
your second journey
whose names you quite forget

On the throat of doors
the ocean hears you
you've touched its blue
you've touched it
and touched it

Is it voices?  It's voices
the color of yesterday
perhaps even before
it is simply the coming
of memory

You knock repeatedly
you tug your coatline
the fine thread
in the eye of buttons
you say, how touching!

No one repeats after you
the color of touch
you've come home
to the color of what

## BHARATA NATYAM DANCER

jana jan was the sound of the dancer's feet
dana dan was the sound of the accompanying
 drum
and the occasion was the inauguration of the
 city hall
and the dancer was the daughter of the
 famous court dancer
who was too well known to be named.

the people applauded
because the ministers applauded.

was she a dancer
or the cousin of an elephant
no one dared to wonder
for she was the daughter of her famous
 mother
who was decorated by many rajahs and
 noblemen
who had gone to america as cultural repre-
 sentative of the country
who was a great social hostess
who had many friends and relatives in the
 government.

great dancer, said the journalists
that's why we invited her, said the mayor
we always had her mother here, said the
 entertainment committee
should be sent to europe as cultural delegate,
 said the deputy minister for culture
yes, said the minister for finance
I knew her mother . . . said the chief
 minister

and people watched the ministers the mayor
    and the entertainment committee
and nodded their heads in approval
when the ministers the mayor and the
    entertainment committee
nodded their heads

and it was one big nodding of heads
wearing the white cap of the congress party.

# THE BLACK DEITY

To the top of the Mylapur hill,
Bald but for the blooming gul-mohur tree,
I returned remembering the afternoon
I watched its red flowers
Shower on the black stone carving
Of the village deity of rain.

But the hill was cracking,
the tree's burnt branches
Bared the black stone
To the beat of the sun.

The batu birds cruised over
Calling to each other,
The black deity has dried up
The tree's red flowers of honey.

At the village men whispered
Of the black deity's wrath—
Pestilence or death in the family.
The priest counselling sacrifice
Kept glancing at the tree
Where the batu birds stilt-walked.

Now, miles away from the tree,
I have a vision of a posse
With lanterns and axes
Creeping up the hill.

BANGLA (water pipe) DESH

The most ambitious water project of West Bengal
Is now complete.
Each pipe is shared only by two families.
Each family has a separate entrance
And a good view of the burning-ghats.
In this one facing west
A family of five is practicing
Concave and convex sleeping postures,
In that one children rotate after a fat fly.
I'm sorry the refugee in this one
Is going through Karmic convulsions. . .

      tearing through
            the mud like stampeding cattle
   carrying all they possess
            on the platform of their heads
Bengalis unnecessarily gifted away in the name of democracy
            have come back
   to their misunderstood country

   faces whose eyes recede
       so far back into terror
   inspect my greeting hands for guns. . .

How many?  Oh so many
Just imagining will crack your nerve,
But these are the lucky who fled
The Pakistani panzers & artillery. . .
This woman has gone crazy,
They threatened to nail her infant to the wall,
When done with her
They nailed the infant anyway. . .

        if all the water-pipes are joined
            a Bangla-tunnel is formed
    the tunnel-nation can surface for necessities
        rationed puffs of air
                    drip-drops from an exhausted tap. . .


perhaps that will please the big powers
            who abhor foreign wars. . .


Here come the ambassadors—
The ambassador of the U.S.A. controls
The umbilical cord of the poor,
Bow to him with highest priority.
The Chinese ambassador is an expert of whispers,
So expert that one ear has to run across
The chest of many nations to hear
What he whispered in the other.
The goat-eyes is from the U.S.S.R.,
He'll herd cadavers together
And march them to a Siberian pasture.
The United Nations is manned by this faceless one
Who keeps shifting his legs.

The rest of the world is a believing mouth
Living obedient dying obedient.
Show the ambassadors in which tunnel you're best hunted
And they'll show you where the food packages are hidden. . .

Jyotirmoy Datta

## PARTING BY THE RIVER

All else remained the same
the boat's reflection shivered as it does
when water is tickled by the wind
and if the stork switched legs
it was hardly unusual

still it seemed to me everything
was falling over
coming unhinged
as when at a fruit stall a single orange
yanked off the bottom by a hasty hand
can make the entire glorious pyramid fall

## TREACHEROUS OBJECTS

There are deceitful objects around us
the needle that pierces
in order to unite
the two blades of the scissors
that seem to make war on each other
to rip open the trusting cloth
the magnetic can-opener
that disembowels the can
to embrace the lid
I would rather have a dagger on my table
it is an honest thing

## THREE PUZZLES

From a secret list
of the puzzles I ponder on
I hereby make public
three

first the fruit, *kamranga,*
or, literally, "desire-red,"
its indented shape
puzzling boyhood taste
colour
green when raw
a pale transparent yellow
when ripe
never red
but it is the one fruit
which is so shaped
that it can embrace
another *kamranga*

when I peel an onion can the peeling
ever really end
or I stop because my misting eyes
are blind to the ever
thinner layers
there is no convincing reason
for an onion to end
it is like a mirror before a mirror
by peeling who ever reached
the final center
the marrow
of an onion

I am terrified by the thought
of a mirror's back
the rear of a mirror
is usually dark
always dull
an expiation for the brightness
of the front
everyone stares at the facade
no one has peered into the heart
of a mirror
I have never caught anyone
contemplating its rear

the thought of the back
is so chilling
one is tempted to laugh it away
with some such joke
as that the back is to the front
the self-effacing wife
of a brilliant egotistic
statesman
the most one is willing to concede
is that the back is a necessary
foundation
of the mirror's brilliancy
as when you have a palace
lighted towers
domes
there have to be dungeons
whips
fires to heat
branding irons

but the idea of a mirror
is more terrifying than of dungeons
mirror being
the opposite of water

true
water too
is transparent
water too
reflects
but water flows
takes any shape
and if it reflects trees or clouds
it is only to draw a protective curtain
on the vulnerable mysteries of the fish
but between the rear and front of a mirror
is an infinite sky with room enough
for the sun and moon and the stars
and yet it is wholly inaccessible
inhospitable to life

Adil Jussawalla

## from MISSING PERSON

### Part I, Section 3

A        's a giggle now
but on it Osiris, Ra.
An 3t's an er . . . a cough,
once spoking your valleys with light.
But the a's here to stay.
On it St. Pancras station,
the Indian and African railways.

That's why you learn it today.

Look out the school at the garden:
how the letter will happen
the rest of your life:
bright as a butterfly's wing
or a piece of tin
aimed at your throat:
expansive as in 'air',
black as in 'dark',
thin as in 'scream'.
It will happen again and again —
in a library in Boston,
in a death-cell in Patna.
And so with the other twenty-five letters
you try to master now — 'cat', 'rat', 'mat'
swelling to 'Duty', 'Patience', 'Car'.

Curled in a cortical lobe (department of languages),  ,
an unspeakable family gibbered.
'Where is their tape?' abroad, at a loss,
he asks. 'What does it say?'

'Wiped out,' they say.
'Turn left or right,

there's millions like you up here,
picking their way through refuse,
looking for words they lost.
You're your country's lost property
with no office to claim you back.
You're polluting our sounds.  You're so rude.'

Get back to your language,' they say.

Part I, Section 8

A mill of tubercular children
is what he wears.
The wretched of history storm into,
they smash
his house of ideas.

Who puffed up an Empire's sails
still fuel the big-power ships,
still make him fly
high to jet-setter fashion.
Blood tumbles down sleeves
hung upside down
to dry
in his flat.

He'll wreck himself yet;
docked in a bar with a criminal friend,
his shirt wrapping him like a wet
sail, his wood carcass breaking and burning
in mutinous sweat.

Part II, Section 6

He was the bloodied parts
that thumped the ground
around a rope that went into the sky.

He was a crowd of tourists
waiting for his own reappearance.
He was an eye in a maze
of its own making that I
could never catch.
He is what slipped out
from under a magic shroud, leaving
a knife pinned in a pumpkin head
to freeze a poor man's blood
behind a shock that said,
'He's acting out my life.
And I want more.'

What bit-parts, what a fall
for one we thought had gone
proud to adventure —
a local astronaut, no less.
How embarrassingly bad his re-entry
in drabs and dribbles,
meaningless symbols,
or that sudden tumult of blood
that messed us all.
Did he foul things up, up there?
It's not very clear.
Still . . .
does anybody here
know of a school of mystics,
a law of optics,
mathematics,
or even one of his odious
street-corner friends
to produce him before
his grieving wife,
our rifles,
or a criminal court of law?

Arun Kolatkar

# THE RAILROAD STATION

1 : the indicator

a wooden saint
in need of paint

the indicator
has turned inward
ten times over

swallowed the names
of all the railway
stations it knows

removed its hands
from its face
and put them away
in its pockets

if it knows when
the next train's due
it gives no clue

the clockface adds
its numerals

the total is zero

2 :  the station dog

the spirit of the place
lives inside the mangy body
of the station dog

doing penance for the last
three hundred years under
the tree of arrivals and departures

the dog opens his right eye
just long enough to look at you and see
whether you're a man a demon a demigod

or the eight-armed railway timetable come
to stroke him on the head
with a healing hand

and to take him to heaven
the dog decides
that day is not yet

3 :  the tea stall

the young novice at the tea stall
has taken a vow of silence

When you ask him a question
he exorcises you

by sprinkling dishwater in your face
and continues with his ablutions in the sink

and certain ceremonies connected
with the washing of cups and saucers

4 :  the station master


the booking clerk believes in the doctrine
of the next train
when conversation turns to, time
he takes his tongue
hands it to you across the counter
and directs you to a superior
intelligence

the two-headed station master
belongs to a sect
that rejects every timetable
not published in the year the track was laid
as apocryphal
but interprets the first timetable
with a freedom that allows him to read
every subsequent timetable between
the lines of its text

he keeps looking anxiously at the setting sun
as if the sunset was part of a secret ritual
and he didn't want anything to go wrong with it
at the last minute
finally he nods like a stroke
between a yes and a no
and says

all timetables ever published
along with all timetables yet to be published
are simultaneously valid
at any given time and on any given track
insofar as all timetables were inherent
in the one printed
when the track was laid

and goes red
in both faces
at once


5 :  vows

slaughter a goat before the clock
smash a coconut on the railway track
smear the indicator with the blood of a cock
bathe the station master in milk
and promise you will give
a solid gold toy train to the booking clerk
if only someone will tell you
when the next train is due


6 :  the setting sun

the setting sun
touches upon the horizon
at a point where the rails
like the parallels
of a prophecy
appear to meet

the setting sun
large as a wheel

Shiv K. Kumar

## AFTERMATH

After a pneumatic bout of love,
lashing our diabetic bodies
to a semblance of orgasm,
we sank deflated into some
      small talk of Zen Buddhism,
      willing to let detachment
      claim our yet unborn,
      to spray napalm over
luscious paddy fields,
or make dentures for spinsters.
      She stirs again, but 1
      see a cockroach creeping up the bedpost.

# A BARREN WOMAN

The flaming magnolia leaves
only tease the blood
in her womb
   that clatters like
   an empty thought
   in an agnostic's mind.
Amidst each night-ploughing
she sees him
bending over her
   with the young offshoot's red eye
   straining hard its muscles
   to burst into new life.
Oh, the monotony of
large male hands
kneading her body.
   Only the toothless gums
   at the mother's founts
   will turn water into wine.

Arvind Krishna Mehrotra

## KABIR'S LAST ENTRY

> As they argued together, Kabir appeared
> before them, and told them to lift the
> shroud. . . They did so, and found in place
> of the corpse a heap of flowers.
> > Evelyn Underhill, Introduction to
> > *One Hundred Poems of Kabir*

The sky, the sky, look I wear it like a sola hat
I sit in the verandah all day
Classifying dreams into mammals and reptiles
Just as Rip Van Winkle tried out ornithology.
My beard's uncombed. When you get to the city
— how should I describe it? —
Ask anyone at the gate, any schoolboy, maid, cobbler
They know the house. At this time of year
The flies go about their business
Like professional soldiers, the dust
Settles on you the minute you arrive and the heat
Phew! I'll go blind. The trees are green
And filled to the brim with crows
Heavy-looking parrots, an occasional monkey.
The zoo for a neighbour. Could you ask for more?
Well there isn't a thing to eat in this house.
Some ginger, garlic, salt, an onion or two
But tomorrow everything might change
The smuggler can turn up with almonds
For the old man, or the retired station-master
With a jackfruit. I've decided to keep the soapdish.
The cloth doll is up for auction
It has red beads for eyes, a smudged mouth
And three pointed fingers. The notebooks
Have come apart, do you want them? They contain data
On calenders, divers systems of medicine, the transformation
Of common objects into inexplicable events.

The bus station is near Zero Road. On Friday afternoons
I visit the bone-setter's widow, her amulets are effective
Against theft. You're surprised. My foolscap
Is still unaccounted for, my walking stick was taken
From behind the cupboard, I worry about the cockroaches
And the pigeons will be displaced
Because those fellows won't finish the roof.
Mishap after mishap; it's getting worse.

The paperweight. Only the other evening
While I worked with that fine set of tools
Given me by an Afghan trader, it slipped and broke.
Nothing was left of the blue palm tree.
It's strange how desperate rebels surrender
To omens; I can see what will happen.
This outpost has been mine for years
And I know, like my own backyard, all the boundaries
That lie between the Khyber and the big delta —
The desert and the shifting hills
The kind Muslim weaver and his wife
The only inseperables, a pair of shoes. Footsteps,
I'd better go now; after all
Even a recluse is unprepared for the anonymity
Of grave-clothes. The rose,
Asks Kabir, is it a serious flower?

# A DEAD MAN LOOKS AT THREE THINGS

## At Poetry

My eyes reflect a hill
of small white bones.
My friends
who come looking for me
disturb a colony of ants.
A black cat
crosses my path.
Actually, I'm not dead
but as if dead.  Out of such
pretensions are poems made.
My relief is comparable
to the old man's finding
his lost coat
or to his coming upon a bench
after a long walk.
Life was kind and left me
two surprises, poetry and my body.

At Himself

Even little things can kill.
Look at me, I was murdered
by language.
Words came up to me
firing from close range
I never knew where the weapons
were concealed.
Some rules I was given
and many more imagined,
these were shells
embedded right under the skin.

Exclamation marks
drilled holes through my knees.
I couldn't take in that violence
Music fell upon me
and I fled
chained in rhythm,
my temples hissed
and the snake took my vein
in his narrow jaw
and sucked the poison.
I still hear the cold skin shiver
pressing against me.

At The Future

Only fools look ahead.
The coward-wise live
by recollection.
Memory travels along its own edges.
Pictures turn up
like the waters.

> The sky and wind
> are curtains
> caught in a window

> Snow
> resembling soldiers
> of once upon a time
> guards the earth

> Warriors
> singing elegies
> bury each other

The last Siberian birds
migrate
to a forest
surrounded by tribes
naked as bows

# SONGS OF THE GANGA

### 1

I am Ganga
Snow from the mountains
The keeper of water

I am the plains
I am the foothills
I carry the wishes of my streams
To the sea

I am both man and woman

I am paper boats for children
I am habits for fishermen
I am a cloud for shaven monks
I reflect all movements

I am the bridge
I am the fort and the archer
Taking aim
I am the great dissolver of men

I give life and I take it back

## 2

I go out into the world
I am the world
I am nations, cities, people
I am the pages of an unbound book

My room is the air around me

I am dressed in water
I am naked as water
I am clarity

A friend comes along
Offers me a flag
And says a government has toppled

I am going to catch rain, I say
And spread out a net

I am poison


## 3

Billy goats
Come down from the mountain
Without finding solitude
Camels return from the desert

I make two lines in the sand
And say they are unbreakable walls

I make four directions one
I know the secret of walking

I am the death of fire

4

From smoke I learn disappearance
From the ocean unprejudice

From birds
How to find a rest house
In the storm

From the leopard
How to cover the sun
With spots

In summer I tend watermelons
And in flood I stay
Near the postman's house

I am a beggar
I am a clown
And I am shadowless

Jayanta Mahapatra

DAWN

Out of the dark, it whirls back
into a darkly mysterious house.

Is it the earth within?
Does it keep us waking, give brief respite?

Like a hard crossword puzzle
it sets riddles against one another:

the thunders trailing around hatchet-faced banana leaves,
a front gate limp with dew,

the acid sounds of a distant temple bell,
the wet silent night of a crow that hangs in the first sun.

Is the dawn only a way through such strange terrain?
The frenzy of noise, which a silence recalls

through companions lost, things suddenly found?
There is a dawn which travels alone,

without the effort of creation, without puzzle.
It stands simply, framed in the door, white in the air:

an Indian woman, piled up to her silences,
waiting for what the world will only let her do.

# THE WHOREHOUSE IN A CALCUTTA STREET

Walk right in. It is yours.
Where the house smiles wryly into the lighted street.
Think of the women
you wished to know and haven't.
The faces in the posters, the public hoardings.
And who are all *there* together,
those who put the house there
for the startled eye to fall upon,
where pasts join, and where they part.

The sacred hollow courtyard
that harbours the promise of a great conspiracy.
Yet nothing you do
makes a heresy of that house.
Are you ashamed to believe you're in this?
Then think of the secret moonlight of the women
left behind their false chatter,
perhaps their reminding themselves
of looked-after children and of home:
the shooting stars in the eager darkness of return.

Dream children, dark, superfluous;
you miss them in the house's dark spaces, how can't you?
Even the women don't wear them—
like jewels or precious stones at the throat;
the faint feeling deep at a woman's centre
that brings back the discarded things:
the little turnings of blood
at the far edge of the rainbow.

You fall back against her in the dumb light,
trying to learn something more about women
while she does that she thinks proper to please you,
the sweet, the little things, the imagined;
until the statue of the man within
you've believed in throughout the years
comes back to you, a disobeying toy—
and the walls you wanted to pull down
mirror only of things mortal, and passing by:
like a girl holding on to your wide wilderness,
as though it was real, as though the renewing voice
tore the membrane of your half-woken mind
when, like a door, her words close behind:
"Hurry, will you?  Let me go,"
and her lonely breath thrashed against your kind.

D. Parameswaran

## UNTITLED

I

I have agreed with the ghosts &
I am a ghost dance
-ing.
Ghosts are happy with me.
Now they'll do anything
I ask, and
I'd give them anything
they want.

The task is big
breaking the continuity string
tied in the distant stars.
They will ask
Give us your heart
Give us your mind
We'll like to play with it.
and I'll give
for I myself am a ghost
dancing.

II

On the moonlit
windows shadow on
the floor in my room.
I place my feet
letting the shadows
darken my feet & get
on the skin.
My eyes look big, into dark
My eyes are white
I am a ghost dance-
ing.

Gieve Patel

## JUST STRAIN YOUR NECK

The tarmac outside my clinic
Flows thick, and befogged spirits
Drop in on me, demanding
A simple, eternal whisk to safety.

"A large city", she says, "but to me
It offers no place to sleep."
Woman so impossible that one by one
Father, friend, brother, and husband
Have let her adrift.

She speaks across my tableful of quiet drugs,
But the tablets quiver inside their factory packages.

The sexual odour of rejected women overpowers me.
I am called grotesquely to account
For ecstacies they may have missed.
I am a chameleon about to swallow a naseous butterfly.
Look, I'm turning green.

To the gods that manage eggs and seeds
I have to say:
The four winds are in your control.
Who and what would you blow
At me with needs
That will not be met? Or why not
shake us up like impersonal blooms
To charge the wind? Then reaching out
To currents of air would be all
The effort needed, the destitute never
To lose heart in their truant healers;
Just strain your neck, and catch a waft
Of thriftless benedictions.

## THE ARROGANT MEDITATION

If it's to be after an aeon's meditation
It might as well be now.  Though
How suppliantly true seekers
Can present their case, humility
A sweet ache that sucks the arrogance
Out, making a mighty vacuum
To reel into.  It must come again,
Arrogance, to pack heart space
Impenetrable.  Because this is
No coy lovers' game of give
Or no give; it is snatching of power —
That's the intention!  Who from?
Who in his senses, complete himself,
Need demand of me inspired abjectness?.
Need trammel me about with so much
But no more, insisting I make virtue
Of mere modest gifts as does
The rest of Nature: Trees
Push their way upward, slim and tough,
And heavy boughs that incline down
Do so upon a tense fulcrum,
Like leopards ready
To spring.  Grovelling underground
Tubers acquire volume; and
Trailing plants quickly cover
The earth's surface, rising
An inch, no more, pressing
At each halt needles of root
Into the ground: Hemmed in within limits,
Self-sufficient, allowed a merely just,
Unclamourous space.

## BODYFEARS, HERE I STAND

Bodyfears, here I stand:
A latitude of arms outstretched
Tip to tip, longitudinally
Scalp to toe. Could
Violence performed on me
Register anywhere at all
Outside? Who
Is to say it happened?
After cremation do ashes writhe,
Remember the living body's
Fight? Orbit ashes
Around the moon, fling them at
Planets' faces! To let out pain
Beyond each sensory prison,
Tape record our screams.

## AUDIENCE

Each moment, and moment after moment,
Somewhere, a private act of menace
Is performed.  A thin continuous cry
Hounds the universe, accompanying
The turning earth — a cry
Reborn, reborn, and interred.
When the act of menace is public
A multitude watches the body of
One man subjected
To varieties of pain.  See exhibited a
Knot of muscle with shocking
Patches of hair, and wonder
How his rising cries differ from
Sounds smothered in
A shut room.  Does one tormentor's
Approval as sole witness
Match weight for weight
The shared full-throated applause
Of a crowd made aware for once
Of every sensation
Under its dress?

A. K. Ramanujan

# HAPPINESS:  AFTER SOME ANTHROPOLOGY

I'm happy, sir,
> that shields of painted cane, the
> sociology
> of Anglo-Indian rum,
> wooden drum,
>
> carved human head
> and the xylophone or
> the charisma of brahmins
>
> and the ritual use
> of bark-cloth and silver
> and the two figurines
>
> of the Shaven Ass
> styles of tattooing
> spiders on the waist
>
> of the infertile wife
> or animal masks that grin
> in tiger-moth colours
>
> with white and yellow lines
> round a hole for a mouth
> or masks that simply grin
>
> in olive-green
> among red circles
> for eyes, do not yet
>
> exclude
> a look

at the face
of the happy widow

of our varicose
cook, nor another look

at mushrooms, those
parasol mobs

in the reeking crotch
of rotting timber

bought for my uncle's
very carefully

imagined
houses.

## AH CHAN

After the day's work
as she sits in the garden
leg cocked
watching the night buses go by
I wonder what she dreams of
our Ah Chan

What ghosts inhabit
that mind
of which we
know so little
outside
her papaya plants
her mad spells
her four-digit misses

Time-hazed flashbacks
perhaps
of far-off Kwangtung
A young girl
Samfoo newly starched
eyes glazed
but
imagination flushed
with tales of quick fortune
packing
hurriedly packing. . . .

Projected dreams
again
of that longed-for return
wild reunions

noisy dinners
with family and friends
(what's left, that is,
of family and friends)

Or visions of retirement?
Long languorous days
in an easy chair
tucked away some corner
of a quiet Kongsi

But perhaps neither
dream nor vision
just schemes
to ward off that wily nephew
—master of the hard luck tale—
so adept at coaxing her
out of her last dollar

After the day's work
as she sits in the garden
watching the buses go by
I wonder what she dreams of
our Ah Chan

# HOMECOMING

Nothing had changed

Wandering once more
through the village
he ticked them off
one by one
in his mind's inventory

      The old kampong well
      cloistered by trees
      where the fledgling girls
      cocooned in flimsy sarongs
      gathered like thieves
      each morning
      to bathe
      before cock's crow
      before the young men awoke

      The dark teetering huts. . . .

      The flickering oil lamps
      around which the small boys
      pressed
      like moths
      each evening
      to hear the old fisherman's tales

      That source of never-ending wonder
      the fresh water spring
      by the hill
      where the older women
      clutching
      bundles of dirty linen

waited patiently
in straggling queues

Those shallow broken drains
of stagnant water
mosquito larva
ribbons
of children's excreta

Controversy rages
A skirt rustles
Differences vaporise

No filigree of words
can pin
your little presences
coiled
in the interstices
of my bone. . .

Spiralling out
to press
against my brain
in your absences

Novels, Friends, Films. . .
A hundred distractions
And still your gnawing absence

Too much pain
Or a concrete heart
This absence of tears.

Wong May

## STUDY OF A MILLIONAIRESS:  STILL LIFE


Pluck away all its fingers and legs.
We want only the crab's face which is its torso,
unbroken mask,
two lashless eyes
signalling
from the quick.

So the  paralyzed old woman
with a big yellow cat on her lap
watches her daughters and grandsons
preparing crabs
for the birthday of the Prosperity Goddess,
who is said to be fond of red.

The youngest peeps into the cauldron,
disillusioned because there isn't
any magic like the green-red apples,
while the cat sits washing its face,
patient like any God-child,
moistening its fishy eyes.

So the paralyzed old woman
watches her daughters and grandsons
eating crabs (from their nails).
The aged is supposed to be like the Goddess,
to be feasted and fed on the colour of the heart,
while the two lashless eyes,
signalling and signalling,
are red and tired.

*Pakistan*
Zulfikar Ghose

EGYPT


Descending towards Cairo, an arid
plain is like a twisted mirror, its haze
the diffused image of the sun.  Egypt
is traw to the sun's flame, its monuments
are slipping into the floodwaters like beasts
come to drink from the dry interior.

Cranes, absurd as science fiction creatures, stand
where slaves once tore their muscles so that kings
might lie entombed in cool, musk smelling darkness,
mummified, perfect as butterfly speciments:
the more advanced a civilization,
the subtler the refinement of vanity.

The same old Egypt holds its sun-wearied earth
together with transfusions from the Nile,
the dammed-up waters a bank of the country's blood.
The concrete lifts its pharoah head above
the people in Cairo, compelling submission
to the hours of work.  The sky is a scrap of iron.

A scholar hurries to a museum,
a tourist points his zoom lens at flies
sticking to a cluster of dates in a bazaar.
Second-hand vision records Egypt, myths
endure.  The same old Egypt contracts like
a dried fig in the heat of the jet's ascent.

Shahid Hosain

## WEDDING

Brightness falls from the air,
From ankle and elbow, from heaving
Gold bosom, curving flash of a knee
Below silk, makes night giddy,
Pastes colour on the muddy unlighted street
Before it falters, plods hesitant in the creak
And shuffle of an unconcerned bullock-cart;
Here it will linger, dispersed
And occupied by the risen dust.

Beneath the shaking lights
Gul Khan the servant is sad;
His stiff martial moustache is sodden
With tears and stolen whisky, he drowns
In grief for the princess the shining doll
Leaving her home for harsh and alien arms.
His pretty plaything, carried for years on his back,
Now lowers her silvered eyes and will not speak.
So Gul Khan the puritan, lecherous Pathan,
Staggers with the parachute sway of the ghararas [1]
And denied the ambit of their tented warmth
Weeps and swigs his stolen whisky,
Placating his anger with unfamiliar fire.

The shining bride is crying
They say, shaking with silent grief,
Huddled and bowed, gold circling her arms,
Lying cold on her forehead, gripping her feet,
The gold-burdened bride is crying,
They tell the groom, appraising him angrily
As he hesitates into a sea of women.

A whisper, a vicarious purr
Of desire crowds the couple as they bend
To the misting mirror.  A meeting of frightened eyes,
A brief ritual of knowledge, broken
By hennaed and jangling hands, a shiver
Of bright laughter, a hum of orthodoxy.
The shehnai's[2] lament, the music of this moment
Coils serpentine, bright, dangerous; familiar sound
Causing familiar sorrow.  The quick taps
Of the tabla lessen, beat resonant and slow
Beneath the young voices singing the final parting.

The doll's wedding is over, they sing, a real groom
Now comes to bruise these pliant, learning arms
To crush her bangles in a strong embrace:
Why have you sold me, father, ask the voices
Into this world of blood and broken glass?

So her mother retreats in grief to elaborate sorrow,
Her father blesses her with a shower of small coins
And she stumbles, besieged by petals to the car
Whose metal hides under jasmine and marigold,
Whose headlights blaze, whose Japanese bugle horn
Sounds merrily through the reducing dust.

Crows snap across the moon-darkened sky
And as usual the children gather with catapults,
Their pockets bulging with smooth round stones,
Waiting the final settling of the birds.
Their mothers shout abuse, but they are tired
And there are so many children.[3]

[1] The *gharara* is a wide floor-length dress, rather like the
crinoline, now worn mostly on formal occasions.

2 The *shehnai* is an instrument similar in appearance and sound to the clarinet, traditionally played at weddings.

3 Most Pakistani weddings still observe the custom of 'arsi mus-haf', in which the bride and groom are supposed to have their first glimpse of one another, by looking into a mirror held between them.

Maki Kureishi

## THE FIRE TEMPLE

A well in the courtyard serves
clear water to rinse the hands
and face of worshippers who make
an invocation, twining the thin
girdle of lamb's-wool between
pious fingers.  Then we go in

and exchange shoes for carpets, sleek
as cat's fur, that dissuade our soft soles
from hard earth.  In the caged centre
of the room, like a circus tiger
the fire rears from a giant urn.
Masked priests and smells of sandalwood

add atmosphere.  Retired men,
earnest and ceremonious, hitched
into window-seats mutter
their daily turnover; two small
girls, in flat, embroidered caps,
wriggle and giggle through their prayers.

Water, lamb's-wool and fire are
artifacts of cattlemen who saw
their bright God season with grain
and mammals a generous earth.
A faith ancient and catholic
as shared bread.
Look how we worship now.

The lamb's-wool girdle sanctifies
bellies of cashiers and tycoons
whose god supplies double entry files.
A high wall crusted with jagged glass
circumvents the temple.  No one
intrudes without shedding blood.


## STATUE OF BRAHMA

> Circa 6th Century A.D. Found Brahmanabad,
> Sind.


No worshipper made this god;
the body's swagger,
its hint of clothing not meant to cover
arrogant thighs.
Look how the torso
indulgently fleshed, rises to four stern heads.
Thought unfolds the austere line
of brow and nose.  Eye
proportioned to a dancer's calm, remote
from banal gesture.  To which
shall we pin faith,
the sensual body or ascetic face?
Art's delicate alibi
hookwinks dogma,
and this god one may worship doubting,
who borrows for Self-beatitude
the carnal metaphor.
All prayer translates into a human form.

## SHALL WE DROWN THE KITTENS

There are too many kittens.
Even the cat is dismayed
at this overestimation
of her stock and slinks
away.  Kind friends cannot adopt
them all.  Some will have to go.

My relatives say: Take them
to the bazaar and let them find
a destiny.  They'll live
off pickings.  But they
are so small, somebody may
step on one, like a tomato.

Or fastidious of spoiling a polished
shoe, kick it out of his path.
Should they live through the gaunt dogs
and battering heels,
they will starve gently, squealing
a little less each day.

The European thing to do
is drown them.  Warm water
is advised to lessen the shock.
They are so small it
takes only a minute.  You hold
them down and turn your head away.

They are blind and will never know
you did this to them.  The water
recomposes itself.  Between
my two cultures which
shall I choose?  I lie awake nights
pondering which is more ethical.

Kaleem Omar

## POEM FOR MY FATHER

Father, it was thirteen years ago
That we buried you among thorns
In a dusty graveyard.  My brother and I
Were out at sea after bloaters
The day you died.  When the boat came in
The news of your death sprang at us
From the mouth of a distant relative
Waiting at the dock to take us home.
I remember noticing, as we rang for the car,
How hot the sun still was on our backs.

The room in which your large body lay,
Covered by a single inadequate sheet,
Was a murmur of familiar faces
Made strange by third person repetitions
Of your name.  My old grandmother renewed
Her grief upon the hollows of your shroud;
Cousins, sisters, brothers, a whole clan,
Shadowed a fallen view of the man
And were unnerved for the first time
Without the affection of your certain hand.

The funeral still rests in the minds of those
Left to mourn the dreams you made so real
That nothing seemed quite impossible.
I remember how we would sit quietly
And listen, hour after hour, to your plans
For offering to build the new Aswan Dam
Or schemes for a house in which the large,
Now scattered family would again
Gather each year over winter holidays.
There would be a special room for children.

And in the same compound you would build
Five cottages for your sisters and their broods.
All would be gathered in again to grow
Up knowing each other as families should know
The smaller parts that make the larger whole.
Your presence held these promises together
And kept our laughter from ringing false.
Now, we plunge headlong on our separate ways
With all the discord of runners out of breath.
Much more than one man perished in that death.

Thirteen years later, my young brother is
Half a stranger in another country.
Two of your four brothers and a sister
Are also dead.  Another brother and a sister
Live with the aftermath of heart attacks.
The family business continues to slide
Downward to a fast approaching end.
Two marriages have broken up; others
Are quarrelling.  A full catalogue of woe.
Father, accept us — we have nowhere else to go.

# A HOUSE DIVIDED

When they occupied the house in Sialkot,
After half a Continent had foundered,
Beds were still laid out,
The cupboards full of things
Carefully hoarded over the years.
In the old fashioned kitchen upstairs
A fried egg burning to a crisp
Had been left in the frying pan.  All signs
Pointed to a frantic departure,
But the rooms, at least, looked solid.

Later, when they had settled in,
The master mason and the carpenter
Who built the house would come
Looking for odd jobs to do
And tell of how the Hindu whose house it was
Had conceived it as a labour of much love.
Nothing but the best teak
For the woodwork, the walls of a thickness
That would last and discourage
The robber on dark winter nights.

And from an old maidservant,
The last one left of those who served
The owners then, they would hear,
In tones of domestic disbelief,
Descriptions of the final scene
That day in ninteen forty seven
On which whole populations fled.
The husband assembling his children
In the courtyard below;
The wife, like one demented,

Clinging to the pillars
When it was time to leave,
Begging the others to go without her.
It is not, no matter how great the fear,
Easy to leave forever
The place of one's birth, the sights
And sounds one will never know again,
The familiar stone of walls
Designed to contain
Several generations of love.

All gone in an instant.  But what of them
Who came to replace
Those who had left?  Did they not feel
A peculiar strangeness
At being refugees in their own
Home town?  For it was from Sialkot
That they had started out,
Following their father's business
Wherever it led them,
Tagging the wide landscapes of India.

And over the years prosperity had come
To mean a way of life,
An accommodation of climate moving on
Whenever there was money to be made.
But when the end came
They too were unprepared
And like a million others had to make
A run for their lives
Without so much as one bedding roll
To spread some warmth between them.

With nothing of their own, they slept
The first few nights
On sheets and pillows sent by relatives
Who had never been anywhere, preferring
The safely multiplying life
To the lucrative unknown.  This lack
Of curiosity, some wisely nodded now,
Had stood those who never moved
In good stead, as if one quiet death
Redeems communal blood.

And India was given separate names
And in a hundred other widely spaced towns
Sad migrations laboured to renew
The roots of love.  So when they came
To the house bequeathed to them
Involuntarily, the Hindu's possessions were
Distributed to the poor.  Now, sickness
Or old age have claimed some of them
And the dumb walls have grown
Familiar enough to be called home.

# REFUGEE

I have lived five years
with the history of this city
and rulers constantly at war.
The walls of its past are now familiar
and I do not need
guide-books to impress the foreigner.

My knowledge of the local dialect
may be uncertain, but at least
I have the swear words pat.
This, in itself, is an accomplishment
not easily laughed at.

As a consequence, I rarely feel
out of place or ill at ease.  So what
if I am a refugee
and suspected of vague disloyalties?

No one can say I have not tried
to fit into the civic scene.
I support all the right charities —

if not with money, then with prayer —
and do not have too much to fear.

But I cannot imagine being buried here.

Taufiq Rafat

## KARACHI

The screaming winds transplant the soil
Particle by particle, the roar of the sun
Is silenced by distance, but its muscular rays
Crack the most stubborn rock like a nut.
And, yes, the sea: biting into the beach head
With an ancient rasping sound.  All the forces
Of nature crowding man off his perch
So that the land can return to its ways.

In this city of scarce sweet water and little rain
Each man protects his plot of greenery
With panicked care.  The municipality plows
The heart of the road for a strip of grass,
And jealously counts its trees on week-days.
The bald sparrow scrounges in the dust-bin;
Only the spendthrift gul-mohur spills its gold
In the pitiful spring that time allows.

We wear our features to suit the landscape;
And malice moves like a rainless cloud
Over the chalk cliffs of the teeth.
From opposite the terminus I stare
At the commuters storming the gates, and see
Where the roof bulges the effeminate rise
Of a dune, and where the lamp-post stands
The arms of the cactus lifted in prayer.

# MONKEYS AT HARDWAR

One remembers the monkeys at Hardwar,
in the good old days when Bharat was India,
who snatched food from the hands of the unwary.
Being sacred, they plundered with impunity.
We were children then, on our way to Lahore
for the winter break.  When we passed Hardwar
we anticipated the monkeys, who perched
in rows on the train-roof awaiting their chance.
We could not see them, but knew they were there
from experience, more sudden and dangerous
than those who chattered on the crowded platform.
There were temples too.   Since then, in my mind,
monkeys and temples have been synonymous.

> The only monkeys one sees now
> are in the zoo, or at the end of a chain,
> but they are a poor lot compared
> to those bold, religious monkeys.

One also remembers, with a twinge of regret,
lone Englishmen in first-class carriages,
remote and godlike, and firmly entrenched
behind three-month old newspapers from Home.
They kept their teeth clenched on cold pipes
as they carried Empire to ungodly districts.
Even in the hottest weather their glass-windows
were shut; they took no notice of the monkeys.
Whenever we wanted to appear superior
we imitated their Ur-doo, and secretly lusted
for the memsahibs who came to kiss them goodbye.
They were clean solid fellows in sola hats
who knew how to keep us out of their hair.

The only sahibs one sees now
are the back-slapping oil executives, .
or the sleazy christs from Europe
who infest our zebra-crossings.


## COMING DOWN FROM THE MOUNTAINS


Coming down from the mountains where everything
Is cool and clean
To the obscene
Flatness of the plains, we discern how

The dictatorship of the tropical sun
Has brought these
Men to their knees
Time and time again.   Alexander was

By no means the first of the conquerors.
Some tribe without
Women or food
Trudged up and peered over the Northwest hills

And saw the amazing greenness and the temples
With real gold tips;
It licked its lips
And came swooping down to begin a trend

Which has not yet ended, perhaps.   Only
Is no longer
Loot or hunger
Which drives them, nor is the North-West

The sole source of danger.  Russia, India,
China are hot
Or friendly; but
We know their looks.  This is our history.  So

Like a tethered goat we wait for the next
Marauder.
With the radar
Cage we turn this way and that, sniffing,

Anticipating the sequent gambit, and
While we wait, are
Much too aware
Of the vulnerable sap that floods our veins.


## 5000 YEARS OF PAKISTAN

This mound, barely thirty feet high,
Which could be comfortably fitted
Into half a football field,
Is all that survives, they tell me.
Of a town 5000 years old.

Archaeologists say the town
Had a highly-developed culture.
The fragments of pottery, painstakingly joined,
And tools littering the museums
Indicate the skill of its craftsmen.
Potter's wheel, grain-jar, plough-share,
And the many ornaments and beads
(Not a weapon in sight)
Prove they were a peace-loving people,
Tillers of the soil, sculptors, artisans,
Who had no use for moats and palisades,
Their only enemy the drought.

But this is mere hypothesis.
The historian has by-passed the mound
For some reason known to himself.
The fastidious hands of the excavator
Have not yet re-constructed here
Another Mohenjo Daro.
To the unpractised eye
The occasional outcrop of slim bricks,
A type no longer in fashion,
Is the sole evidence of its antiquity.

Still, they are all there, I suppose:
The wide lanes and sensible houses,
And a marvellous system of drainage
That did not poison the rivers and the sea,
And miracle of miracles
Only the one temple for the populace.

What cold-eyed bravoes from the North
On restive horses, desolated them,
Only the wind knows.

On the top
Of the knoll a banyan tree
Protects the giant grave from the sun;
While endless acres of water-logged fields
Have pushed to its very hem
A village of two-score houses of mud;
A sluggish drain runs down the middle
Into which all the children defecate.

# CARIBBEAN

# INTRODUCTION

## THE DIVIDED SELF — EUROPE VS. AFRICA

A problem which has faced the Caribbean is that of the divided self. Whatever the skin colour of the Caribbean creole, he/she has had to see in himself/herself a bit of the Caribbean, a bit of Africa, and a bit of Europe. The proportions vary, allegiances change as time passes, but confusion remains, ever complex, ever baffling. In an effort to simplify this maze of complexities, Caribbean man has from time to time looked to Europe, rather than to Africa. Europe has been the source of inspiration, of progress; identifying with Europe has been seen to offer hope for a solution.

Some white creoles, not satisfied with their position of privilege in Columbus' West Indies, have journeyed to England especially, to refresh their whiteness, to put an extra coat on to maintain its splendour, and so at least maintain their station or improve it, on their return. Nearly all, if not all, found that their whiteness was different from the "home" whiteness of the "Mother Country". Some were extremely upset about this, others less so, and others accepted their lot. On their return they all learnt the lesson, that it was preferable to be big white fish in the small multi-coloured Caribbean pond. Some stayed in a determined effort to achieve the Mother Country's whiteness. A few were unfortunate, and were consumed by the new problem. In later years, some of those who returned were disappointed to find that as a product, their market value had diminished and that the future was not very promising. Here was another problem. How would they solve the new one. To become more Caribbean would mean becoming more African. The new problem was more complex.

There were some black creoles who, although conscious that they could not become white outwardly, thought or were encouraged to think that inwardly the colour of their black souls could be lightened to the point where the cleansed inner rays would shine through their black skins and elevate them to a level above their fellows. Some may have thought that with continuing assiduity, they would eventually look their former masters in the eye. There is no doubt that in some cases, the market value of these black creoles increased, but in later years this was not the case. Some of them found, on their return, that as a product, they were not wanted, that what they had discarded was in demand. Could they return to this? Here was a new problem.

In recent years there has been a "back to Africa" movement, not so much in a geographical sense, but in a spiritual sense. Our supporters have been journeying to an Africa which many travelers say does not exist, and which in the opinion of some historians, never existed. Another problem for the self of Caribbean man. Some critics claim the Caribbean man has slavishly accepted the Black Americans' Africa of the dashiki, the Afro and the beads. The web thickens as the net widens.

So what is the Caribbean self? A three flavoured brick ice-cream of Europe, Caribbean, and Africa in the Caribbean? Where in the Caribbean can one find Africa? The self remains divided.

## CARIBBEAN MAN VS. CARIBBEAN MAN

In an attempt to grapple with his big problem, Caribbean man separates it into parts. So he finds that his problem of division has many subdivisions. Islands and mainland territories are divided by water, men and women are divided by chromatic shades, the rulers are divided from the ruled, the have-gots from the have-nots, the university graduates from the rest, and so on, and so on . . . In *"For Certain Demagogues"* Barbados' Hilton Vaughan in a compact, concise and incisive poem uses space, and very effectively, in pointing out the depths to which some politicians will descend in order to prey on "the people" they "love." Guyanese Martin Carter in a longer poem where language flows like the river which as image and symbol depicts the ever moving, ever powerful force of the powers that be constantly threatening the man who, though he knows the odds are against him, is "willing to take the risk . . ." and speak his mind in the language "any fool can understand."

It always happens that sooner or later, the underdog tries to collaborate with his fellows in other territories. This is never easy, even if the boundaries are drawn on earth alone. In the Caribbean, the dividing artist traces his separations in earth and sea. A. L. Hendriks' *Mare Nostrum* does not help the underdog. "A man in his strength might walk / San Francisco to New York" but the Rastafari finds that the Caribbean sea divides, but the Atlantic Ocean joins, this time to Africa: "Mek us unite with Africa / Island man doan' understand we."

The Caribbean has an inter-non-white colour problem. Louise Bennett's *Colour Bar* has a nearer black speaker who is comfortable enough to say "Me sorry fe po' red kin . . .", but who does not want the colour bar to remain open. The last two lines of the final stanza contain an interesting image of medicinal cure: "Me need a dose o' fire / to bun dung de colour bar."

Some observers feel that the inter-colour problem is disappearing rapidly, but the have-gots in the Caribbean are mostly near white. Bongo Jerry's speaker in *Sooner or Later* is black. Rastafarians live in a country where wealth and power are not in the palms of the blacks. One must observe that Bongo Jerry's . . . . rhythms. He uses stresses which are slapped . . . . . . "But mus' . . ./The force? . . . Dem a fake . . . But mus'." and high pitch on the final stress in many of the long lines highlights the deep concern of the speaker for the underprivileged. "Sheep" and "goat" are each four legged, but their similarity ends there. Connotations emphasize the vast difference between them.

In recent years, a comparatively large number of university graduates have been residing in the English speaking Caribbean, most of them products of the University of the West Indies, with its three campuses in Mona, Jamaica, Cave Hill, Barbados and St. Augustine, Trinidad, and with its Entra-Mural centres in each territory, from Belize to Trinidad. A new breed of Caribbean man, they speak aloud, write, demonstrate, comment and criticize. Some of them have paid dear penalties for doing what they felt bound to do, and saying what they felt they had to say (see Martin Carter's *Cuyuni* above). Bruce St. John's *Upstart* is a university graduate whose trend toward iconoclasm is hammered home by the use of anaphora in stanzas and the constant repetition of "power."

Divisions . . . create tension, tension creates rebellion. Rebellion is often destructive, and regressive. In the image of the snake, Derek Walcott's speaker in *A Patriot to Patriots* warns in powerfully biting couplets against the dangers of rebellions which wear the masks of revolutions, of the treachery and betrayal that lurks behind those masks.

## THE PROBLEM SEEN — REACTIONS

Sooner or later one has to react to a problem. One solution that looks simple is running away. *Colonization in Reverse* and *Back to Africa* both by Louise Bennett reflect this action—the former might be thought of as *Back to England* since few blacks can deny that a drop or drops of white blood may be found in their veins. The tone of *Colonization in Reverse* is that of approval, but that of *Back to Africa* is one of ridicule, apparently not because going to Africa is a ridiculous idea: "Go a foreign, seek yuh fortune, / But noh tell nobody sey / Yuh aah-go te seek yuh homelan' / For a right deh so yuh deh!"

There are those who are interested in the cause of the problem; so they look back into time and experience searching for the cause. Edward Brathwaite in the extract from *The Emigrants,* a part of his fine and well known trilogy goes back to Columbus' coming. What did his coming bring to the Caribbean? In the fifth and final stanzas, "Parrots screamed." and "Crabs snapped their claws / And scattered as he walked towards our shore" are more than the simple descriptions they seem to be. The aural imagery of bird and amphibian eloquently declare that the problem began right then and there.

Syl Lowhar's *The Colonial* deals with the English Columbuses, who brought African slaves, while Jagdip Maraj's speaker looks sadly at the plight of indentured "East Indians" in Europe's West Indies. So does Dennis Scott in *Epitaph* where the pendulum image of a hanged slave swings through both stanzas.

Older folks have always been observed, consulted, or even looked up to in times of stress, even in metropolitan Western civilization, which is very good at putting them out of the way, when tension decreases. Shana Yardan's "son"/"daughter" takes a sympathetic look at his grandfather, enshrouded in his dhoti with rice sprouting from his personality in every stanza. In city imagery antithetical to visual and aural imagery of rural areas, one senses the sons' loss in not paying attention to what the old man might offer towards solving the problem they have left behind in space and spirit.

Robert Lee's old man not only evokes sympathy, but admiration, a force which can assist the young in identifying the problem, in finding in African culture a source for strength to continue the struggle. Similarly "Old Rasta" draws admiration for Wayne Brown's speaker in *Rasta Fisherman.* But this admiration does even more, it brings a promise. ". . . all earth shall be / the lion's beach, Ethiopia shining, not this / silly shifting island / of bark . . ."

At times the pressures of life enforce action whether preceded by thought or not. Jaffo sings his way out of the problem, Frank John's first person speaker dances it away, Calypsonian plays it through "the arteries" of his guitar, Elliot Bastien's boys and girls hope to solve it by "living it up," and Tony McNeill's first person speaker smokes it away.

Some of us hope to solve our problems through scapegoats. The sugar cane is one of Caribbean man's scapegoats. Many poems have speakers who attack cane. These persons forget that cane is also creole, and was brought to the Caribbean to be exploited. Ten times as benign as Moses' God, they visit the sins of the colonists on cane, and cane's children, not unto the third and fourth, but up to the thirtieth and fortieth generations. Fortunately, the classical eye of A. N. Forde in *Canes by the Roadside* finds sympathy for cane. So does Margaret Gill when she manipulates the rhythms and cadences of the Barbadian dialect to make *Lovesong of a Cane Cutter* capable of drawing from an all-white audience of artists that silent response which stated that they had not only been reached, but touched as well.

Hesitancy is a reaction to problems. One sees a problem, is eager and able to do and have something done about them; but since others must be involved, one hesitates like the speakers in Andrew Salkey's *Postcard from London, 23.10.72.* The final stanza in lean language, but powerful through the pauses, especially that after the exclamation mark, is doubly critical of self and others.

It is wise not to forget or ignore the past, to face the present squarely but with caution, and to prepare for replacing the future with something better than what is in the present. In *Islands,* Alvin Massy faces the present with a critical eye, ending the poem with a look mindful of the past. Savour this image: "Under the overturned basin of the blue / dishevelled palms bow their heads / to the wind / baring sabred fronds / which rip the celophane daylight," then this: "Transplanted tribes pine in squalor / which seeps its vicissitudes / into the very soul of splintered peoples,". Ian McDonald in *Colour Poem* looks at the present too in many happy colours, but he remembers the harsh colours of the past. The *Hymn-Tunes* is a very interesting poem. Unlike the colonists and colonized, hymn-tunes never became creoles. They journeyed from England to the Caribbean and back, from "Gothic cathedral" to "Low Church" and back again undeveloped, undefiled. So Caribbean man has to write new tunes to creole rhythms, and still reach God. In *Exile,* Dennis Scott's very mature speaker has reached the stage where he can deal with the immediate past by self-examination, self-criticism, and forgiveness. We are on our way to love, probably the only solution to our Caribbean problem.

Love reconciles opposites, it does not ask any one to tell the truth, the whole truth, and nothing but the truth. Love knows this is impossible to man. Love bestows citizenship without passports or oaths. Love has no motives . . . no purposes. The speaker in Frank Collymore's *This Land* loves it with all its antitheses, "Mingling in haphazard and experimental union . . ." For the speaker of *Hymn to the Sea,* the sea is no Mare Lostrum, it is the "Symbol of fruitfulness, symbol of barrenness / Mother and destroyer, the calm and the storm! Royston Ellis finds in *In the Gentle Afternoon* such business ... such activity ... such peace ... in spite of "last night's trouble ... the problems of cross week ... and Kwame Apata glories in sensuous notes of the provocative steel pan. Bruce St. John makes *Trade Winds* citizens of the Caribbean without changing their names, and finally in *Words are the Poem* Frank Collymore invites us to continue our love through poetry.

—Bruce St. John

*Barbados*
Edward Brathwaite

## From THE EMIGRANTS

Columbus from his after-
Deck watched stars, absorbed in water,
Melt in liquid amber drifting

Through my summer air.
Now with morning, shadows lifting,
Beaches stretched before him cold and clear.

Birds circled flapping flag and mizzen
Mast: birds harshly hawking, without fear,
Discovery he sailed for was so near.

Columbus from his after-
Deck watched heights he hoped for,
Rocks he dreamed, rise solid from my simple water.

Parrots screamed.  Soon he would touch
Our land, his charted mind's desire.
The blue sky blessed the morning with its fire.

But did his vision
Fashion, as he watched the shore,
The slaughter that his soldiers

Furthered here?  Pike
Point and musket butt,
Hot splintered courage, bones

Cracked with bullet shot,
Tipped black boot in my belly, the
Whip's uncurled desire?

Columbus from his after-
Deck saw bearded fig trees, yellow pouis
Blazed like pollen and thin

Waterfalls suspended in the green
As his eyes climbed towards the highest ridges
Where our farms were hidden.

Now he was sure
He heard soft voices mocking in the leaves.
What did this journey mean, this

New world mean: dis-
Covery? Or a return to terrors
He had sailed from, known before?

I watched him pause.

Then he was splashing silence.
Crabs snapped their claws
And scattered as he walked towards our shore.


OGUN *(a fragment from 'Islands')*


My uncle made chairs, tables, balanced doors on, dug out
coffins, smoothing the white wood out

with plane and quick sandpaper until
it shone like his short-sighted glasses.

The knuckles of his hands were sil-
vered knobs of nails hit, hurt and flat-

tened out with the blast of a heavy hammer. He was knock-
    knee'd, flat-
footed and his clip clop sandals slapped across the concrete

flooring of his little shop where canefield mulemen and a fleet
of Bedford lorry drivers dropped in to scratch themselves and
    talk.

There was no shock of wood, no beam
of light mahogany his saw teeth couldn't handle.

When shaping squares for locks, a key hole
care tapped rat tat tat upon the handle

of his humpbacked chisel. Cold
world of wood caught fire as he whittled: rectangle

window frames, the intersecting x of fold-
ing chairs, triangle

trellises, the donkey
box-cart in its squeaking square.

But he was poor and most days he was hungry.
Imported cabinets with mirrors, formica table

tops, spine-curving chairs made up of tubes, with hollow
steel-like bird bones that sat on rubber ploughs,

thin beds, stretched not on boards, but blue high-tensioned
    cables,
were what the world preferred.

And yet he had a block of wood that would have baffled them.
With knife and gimlet care he worked away at this on Sundays,

explored its knotted hurts, cutting his way
along its yellow whorls until his hands could feel

how it swelled and shivered, breathing air,
its weathered green burning to rings of time,

its contoured grain still tuned to roots and water.
And as he cut, he heard the creak of forests:

green lizard faces gulped, grey memories with moth
eyes watched him from their shadows, soft

liquid tendrils leaked among the flowers
and a black rigid thunder he had never heard within his hammer

came stomping up the trunks. And as he worked within his
        shattered
Sunday shop, the wood took shape: dry shuttered

eyes, slack anciently everted lips, flat
ruined face, eaten by pox, ravaged by rat

and woodworm, dry cistern mouth, cracked
gullet crying for the desert, the heavy black

enduring jaw; lost pain, lost iron;
emerging woodwork image of his anger.

Frank A. Collymore

## THIS LAND

This the land, this the island,
This the legendary clay of Atlantis
Crowned with fans of coral filigree
Outspread upon the lost realm of the diatom;
This the lonely outpost of an alien new world:
      This the land, our island land.

This spot halfway from anywhere to everywhere,
This barren land, this fruitful land,
This unlikely solitary sister of the Caribbees
That lies low and dim upon the face of the waters,
This sliver of an old world adrift upon a foreign sea:
      This our land, our only land.

This land of pastel tints and compromise,
Of huddled tenantries and garden villages,
Of rumshops and churches, slums and postcard views
This land where sugarcane impersonating wheat
Deceives the traveler's eye, this land
      Often referred to as Little England.

This land where the hibiscus and the oldworld rose,
Timid wild hare and sly mongoose,
Dawdling donkeycart and streamlined Cadillac
Have nodding acquaintance, this land where
Sedgemoor sleeps beside the Guinea Coast;
      This halfway postern, this island.

This land where Africa and Britain meet
In exile, living apart but yet
Mingling in haphazard and experimental union
To produce the unpredictable mixture, inheriting
The pride and arrogance of their fathers and
      the all-sufficiency of the older tribe.

This land of sea-eggs, flying fish, rum
And freshwater springs, hatred and love,
Silver beaches, pullulating population, light
And darkness, is much like any other land,
A credulous land, a sceptical land,
      This little land, our island,

And yet this land, this island land,
This flyspeck limned in pale green
And mottled white upon the everlasting blue,
Possesses her own beauty, beauty that life
Scorns not, yields her womb's increase
      Individual, independent: our land.


## HYMN TO THE SEA


Like all who live on small islands
I must always be remembering the sea,
Being always cognizant of her presence; viewing
Her through apertures in the foliage; hearing,
When the wind is from the south, her music, and smelling
The warm rankness of her; tasting
And feeling her kisses on bright sunbathed days:
I must always be remembering the sea.

Always, always the encircling sea,
Eternal: lazylapping, crisscrossed with stillness;
Or windruffed, aglitter with gold; and the surf
Waist-high for children, or horses for Titans;
Her lullaby, her singing, her moaning; on sand,
On shingle, on breakwater, and on rock;
By sunlight, starlight, moonlight, darkness:
I must always be remembering the sea.

Go down to the sea upon this random day
By metalled road, by sandway, by rockpath,
And come to her. Upon the polished jetsam,
Shell and stone and weed and saltfruit
Torn from the underwater continents, cast
Your garments and despondencies; reenter
Her embracing womb: a return, a completion.
I must always be remembering the sea.

Life came from the sea, and once a goddess arose
Fullgrown from the saltdeep; love
Flows from the sea, a flood; and the food
Of islanders is reaped from the sea's harvest.
And not only life and sustenance; visions, too,
Are born of the sea: the patterning of her rhythm
Finds echoes within the musing mind.
I must always be remembering the sea.

Symbol of fruitfulness, symbol of barrenness,
Mother and destroyer, the calm and the storm!
Life and desire and dreams and death
Are born of the sea; this swarming land
Her creation, her signature set upon the salt ooze
To blossom into life; and the red hibiscus
And the red roofs burn more brightly against her blue.
I must always be remembering the sea.

A. N. Forde

## CANES BY THE ROADSIDE

Time was
you tossed in a delirium
of whispers near the roadside:
now your last whisper
is a treasury of lost sound.

Months ago
you were a handful
of green ribbons teasing the wind:

now dead strips tell
where the colour and the sparkle go.

In the cycle
of things you will submit
to the tyranny of shining teeth
and the remorseless murmur of the mill
and all your once-green pride will not console a bit.

Heaped up
in your pyre ready for
the yearly sacrifices to power
you lie robbed of the majesty
of your plotted earth
bared of the eagerness of your dream.

Margaret Gill

## LOVESONG OF A CANECUTTER

You evah see a cane-cuttah
wid he back ta de win'
an' he bill in han',
while he facin' de cane wid he body tall
an' a smile 'pon he face?

He does touch de cane
        soft an' smooth
like a lover an' smile
while de win' singin'
wid de song o' de shack-shack tree.

Den he does hol' de soil
an' crush it fine,
till it pour thru he han's
like de soft red gold
o' dem Paradise sunsets
that does slip thru yah han's an' yah hair.

Den he's be off,
killin' an' cuttin'
wid he bill swingin'
an' he body singin'
de only song o' love dat he know
de song o' death ta de cane.

See 'e hack de cane
see 'e body curve back
den crack like a whip
as de bill flaṣh down, an' *huh*!
de bill gashin' an tearin' de cane from it roots in de soil —

*huh!* an' bleedin' it life in de sticky blood o' it juice —
*huh!* an' de silent watcher o' de massacre see
an' burn de memory in de cane-cuttah back.

You evah see a cane-cuttah
wid he back ta de cane
when he facin' de road
an' de smile 'pon he face
is he pleasure wid de song he just sing?

Bruce St. John

## UPSTART

I'm not in the least ashamed
Of my title gown nor hood
Whatever your evaluation
They're a sign of my liberation.

> I'm not ashamed of the land of my birth
> Whatever you think of its worth
> I love my people, their language, their food.

Let me criticize them
You laugh at your own
Or laugh at mine with your own
Ridicule devaluates
But do not forget that
Ten minus two exceeds seven.

A society of fools, we're
Ashamed of our past
Ignoring our teachers' example
We've murdered and whored
But so have their sovereigns
And where's our Tower, our
Money earning Monument, our
Archives of villainy and shame?

We continue in the present as we did in the past
Paying homage where none ever was due
We are awed at the mystique robbery
Encased in a collar and tie
When milk out of coffee needs more expertise
Than money from a learned fool's pocket.

Dust to dust, ashes to ashes. . .
        Dust to dust, ashes to ashes. . .
        Antiquated myths crass stupidity
        Rules our lives and foils our wishes.

We still believe that selling is power
We still believe that ruling is power
We still believe that ignorance is power
We even believe that colour is power.

Stop buying and see
Stop rioting and see
Stop learning and see

        Poverty is power
        Dust is power
        Ashes is power
        Death is power

Wind power isn't white
Water power isn't black
Fire power's lots of colour
Love power has no colour

With one underdeveloped exception
All the powers have the power to corrupt,
This power dethrones all other powers,

Will you try it on me or will you
Wait and see
The results, dire results of the
Powers that be?

LIGHTERS


Dead for some time, if wood can die
In sickly green dead water, if water's mortal
Lanky palm trees with broken scabby skin
Watch over your grave with wither'd look.

No one erected you a monument
They left you here to rot.

Around the corner the water's alive,
Huge liners, freighters safely
Tugged into the man-made harbour,
Machines empty and fill their holds,
The atmosphere reeks with progress.
Thanks to enormous shapeless
Boulders lugged from disembowelled quarries,
They have a port, they don't need you.

But I choose you
You are my paradox
Feather that never flew
Half shell of giant snail
With monstrous oars
Fit only for a tropical Cyclops.

Barbados had no Misters then
But only masters of bodies beautiful
Of ebony lit by the glistening
Sweat of honest toil could move you,
Major pectorals deltoids and biceps
Bulged to crowd the wharf
With clothing food and shelter,
Gastrocnemius trapezius and others well defined

Elicited silent awe and smiling admiration
Not boisterous jeers or envious handclaps
Or empty silver trophies.

O solid lightermen
Walking the sunburn plank
Gone to your silent home
But not forgotten
May these dead lighters resurrect you
as the poet dips his tiny paddle
In sea-blue ink, that some of the chosen
May behold, commune with you
Before you vanish, disappear once more.

H. A. Vaughan

## FOR CERTAIN DEMAGOGUES

'We love the people, sir,' You do?
　　You ought to; nay, indeed, you must:
Shouting their needs has brought a new
　　Elation to your fickle dust.

You have the keys of all their hearts,
　　Yet neither charity, good sense,
Nor truth, nor tolerance imparts
　　One sparklet to your eloquence.

You prey, but not like beasts of prey;
　　The cobblers fly too far to be
Your emblem; in a higgling way
　　You have a place in history;

Like blackbirds in their shiny coats
　　Prinking and lifting spry, proud feet,
Bickering and picking sodden oats
　　From horses' offal in the street.

*Belize*
G. Charles

# SONG OF THE CAYE SPIRITS

We are the barracuda's
Teeth:
And we are the bitten
Papaya.
No nymph dies this side of the
Reef:
No cypress lives
To cry her.

We know the avocado
Law:
And our rock is the
Mango cliff.
Soft in the white sand life is
Sure:
And love's answer is never
An "if".

*Dominica*
Royston Ellis

## IN THE GENTLE AFTERNOON

Such commerce
for a small village without a representative
on Central Government, without a village council,
without a working public toilet, with two
stand pipes, three rum shops and a cricket pitch;
such business
as citizens sit on benches and discuss
the latest test scores, last night's trouble
at the dance, Sunday's chance in the rounders match
the price of cod fish, the problems of cross week;
such activity
late in the afternoon on Friday as mother
rushes over to seize her child; boys plot;
a girl shouts her directions, a jeep coughs
to a standstill by the shop, and erupts an eager crowd;
such peace
in the gentle afternoon, as the sun begins to die
and everybody drifts away to attend their affairs
all part of the village family, all private people
with each a share of secrets, known by all.

# IN THE SHADE OF OUR HERITAGE

Great saman tree, branches spread
over a patch of green, an ardent
guardian of a familiar scene — players
watchful around the pitch to catch
a soaring ball — sends shadows, blends colours
of boys in bright shirts, girls in hot pants
nestling like lovers in its arms,
students intent, on benches in its shade;
a majestic fan, sun-mottled in the afternoon,
sweeping above the white screen, sight seen
beside a lonely roller beneath the bushes
of attendant vegetation, as the paceman pauses
before his devastation takes another wicket;
stirs the breeze, waves the trees, leaves —
a gentle rain fall, as the fieldsman leaps
to catch the man out. He goes sadly —
so near his century — the long walk back; tears
which well in his eyes are denied by the cheers
from men of his country proud of his stand
in the shade of our heritage, the great saman.

## THE COLONIAL

From the hollowness of the cave,
I come, the echo of a cry
of pain, the shadow of a slave
whose sole salvation was the grave.

My bone fertilises the earth;
my blood lubricates the machine;
my sweat waters the field: my worth
was predetermined at my birth.

I carve my memory on rock;
preserve my grief in song.
I'm slammed by the racket,
like a shuttlecock,
from this to that imperial block.

Broken in spirit and in frame,
I stand on the verge of tomorrow
with the incubus of my shame,
without identity, without a name.

*Guyana*
Kwame Apata

## NAME CHANGE

I searched,
Hunted in vigilant silence
Among Yoruba, Akan,
West, East African ancestral phones
For sounds that shape your homing spirit, free.
Early this morning,
As chill Den Amstel winds
Flung the branches of tie-dye this side and that,
In a Mashona thicket,
Deep in the cultural foilage,
—Wona, Tichy wona
Caught you, named you,
"We shall see," lame, alien tongue interprets:
Sounds that speak
Of harness'd power making a new thrust;
Tension,
Expectation,
Vitality.

PAN MAN

He crouches
Tense,
Above round suspended webs;
His hands,
Crossed in mystique,
Caress the pair of pans.

Rubber-tipped fingers
Tickle the bubbies
Spread beneath his chest;
Sounds,

Provocative as nipples,
Leap, like a heart,
From the excited notes,
Ripping decorous restraint
That leashes my self to care,

God!

Africa in exile,
Giving life to drums
Of steel.

Martin Carter

## CUYUNI

Inside my listening sleep
a roar of water on stubborn rock
was the whisper of blood in the womb of my mother..
And when I awoke
I began listening again.

Why does water
ever running water of the river
never pause to take a rest on the back of rocks?
Or even on that place God has designed for it
out of the violent marriage of sun and rain and wind
and the birth and death of trees, labour of roots
growing beneath the seeking upward face
of the ever yielding water
which hide the testicles of seasons
in its own and my groin.

It is for this reason and certain others
I have decided to have only an acquaintance
with this ever dropping, ever racing river
and to speak of it in a code
few can measure nearly;
and the unbelievable conclusion is not an ending
but a closing of lips
and to talk about it openly in common places
may well provoke its fury, and in that fury
liberate one of its many demons
and send his anger roaming the void for me.

So then if perhaps in some stupid fit of arrogance
I said something any fool can understand
and this river heard me, and decided on vengeance,

where is one who could give me
weapons I shall be able to use?
some mental arrow, magical spell or dream
to ward away the finger of its immense accusation?

If any of you can I shall be willing to take the risk.
But I must warn you if good advices
prove as useless as a paddle in the falls
you will be happy to be transformed as much as I will have to
by the side of this menacing, sullen river
at the mercy of the swing of hawk sight
as far from the noise of language
where gods still live and brood on thrones of rock.

Roy Heath

## THE WAKE

The room was bursting
From the sound of tambourines
For the mother of mothers
Was dead.
The coffin trembled
Under the purple-lipped head
As the mourners
Looked down in awe.
Pale blue light
Gloved her hands.
She had trodden
Every village-brick
With her naked soles,
Known every house a shell.
As a girl in white silk
She stepped down into a boat
To her marriage
With eyes like wine vessels.

Above the river
There are trees on a hill
Like dry grass

Above the river
winding through our lives
There she bore a harvest
Of children
Who grew old before her.

Where is Shooloo
And Serafine?
A devoted husband
Covered with blossoms
Where mists rise over the water.

The mother of mothers
Seized a sword
To defy death
And an empty house.

An old woman
Sits with her handful of beads
Listening to the dogs
Barking on the porch
And the slow drums.

Shana Yardan

## EARTH IS BROWN

Earth is brown and rice is green,
And air is cold on the face of the soul

Oh grandfather, my grandfather,
your dhoti is become a shroud
your straight hair a curse
in this land where
rice no longer fills the belly
or the empty placelessness
of your soul.

For you cannot remember India.
The passage of time
has too long been trampled over
to bear your wistful recollections,
and you only know the name
of the ship they brought you on
because your daadi told it to you.

Your sons with their city faces
don't know it at all
Don't want to know it.
Nor to understand that
you cannot cease
this communion with the smell
of cow-dung at fore-day morning,
or the rustling wail
of yellow-green rice
or the security of
mud between your toes
or the sensual pouring
of paddy through your fingers.

Oh grandfather, my grandfather,
your dhoti is become a shroud.
Rice beds no longer call your sons.
They are clerks in the city of streets
Where life is a weekly paypacket
purchasing identity in Tiger Bay,
seeking a tomorrow in today's unreality.

You are too old now to doubt
that Hannuman hears you.
Yet outside your logie
the fluttering cane
flaps like a plaintive tabla
in the wind.
And when the spaces inside you
can no longer be filled
by the rank beds of rice,
and the lowing morning
cannot stir you to rise
from your ghoola,
The music in your heart
will sound a rustling sound,
and the bamboos to Hannuman
will be a sitar in the wind.

Jamaica
Louise Bennett

## COLONISATION IN REVERSE

*Jamaicans, who have been migrating since the late 19th century
(to Panama, Central America or the U.S.A.), turned in the
early 1950's to Britain, where some 200,000 first generation
Jamaicans now reside. Truly a paradox of colonial history in
this colonisation in reverse to the Mother Country which once
settled her colonies with Britons who came as planters, traders,
administrators, technicians, etc.*

Poet's Note

Wat a joyful news, Miss Mattie!
I feel like me heart gwine burs';
Jamaica people colonizin
Englan in reverse.

By de hundred, by de t'ousan,
from country and from town,
by de ship-load, by de plane-load,
Jamaica is Englan boun.

Dem a-pour out o'Jamaica;
everybody future plan
is fe get a big-time job
and settle in de mother lan.

What a islan! What a people!
Man an woman, old an young,
jusa pack dem bag an baggage
an tun history upside dung!

Some people don't like travel,
but fe show dem loyalty,
dem all a-open up cheap-fare-
to-Englan agency.

An week by week, dem shippin off
dem countryman like fire,
fe immigrate an populate
de seat o' de Empire.

Oonoo see how life is funny?
Oonoo see de tunabout?
Jamaica live fe box bread
outa English people mout'.

For wen dem catch a Englan,
an start play dem different role,
some will settle down to work
an some will settle fe de dole.

Jane say de dole is not too bad
because dey payin' she
two pounds a week fe seek a job
dat suit her dignity.

Me say Jane will never find work
at the rate how she dah-look,
for all day she stay pon Aunt Fan couch
an read love-story book.

Wat a devilment a Englan!
Dem face war an brave de worse;
but I'm wonderin' how dem gwine stan'
colonizin' in reverse.

# BACK TO AFRICA

The Back-To-Africa movement has its advocates in Jamaica among the Ras Tafari, who believe in the divinity of Haile Selassie, Emperor of Ethiopia, and in the pre-destined repatriation of the "black Israelites" (Jamaican blacks) to the Promised land (Africa and/or Ethiopia). In this poem the aspirations of the movement are seen as a defiance of commonsense and of the realities of the historical situation of the Jamaican people. What a confusion would indeed result, "Ef de whole worl' start fe go back, Weh dem great granpa come from". A final advice is given in the last verse which reflects a common attitude. In other words, there may be some point in migrating to seek one's fortunes, but migrating in search of roots is hardly sensible since Jamaica is home— "....a right deh so yuh deh!" This poem was written in 1947, but belongs in spirit to the Jamaica of the sixties.


Back to Africa Miss Matty?
Yuh noh know wha yuh dah-sey?
Yuh haffe come from some weh fus,
Before yuh go back deh?

Me know sey dat yuh great great great
Gramma was African,
But Matty, doan yuh great great great
Grampa was Englishman?

Den yuh great granmada fada
By yuh fada side was Jew?
An yuh grampa by uh mada side
Was Frenchie parley-vous!

But de balance o'yuh family
Yuh whole generation
Oonoo all bawn dung a Bun grung
Oonoo all is Jamaican!

Den is weh yuh gwine Miss Matty?
Oh, you view de countenance,
An between yuh an de Africans
Is great resemblance!

Ascorden to dat, all dem blue-y'eye
Wite American,
Who-fa great granpa was Englishman
Mus go back a Englan!

Wat a debil of a bump-an-bore,
Rig-jig and palam-pam!
Ef de whole worl' start fe go back
Weh dem great granpa come from!

Ef a hard time you dah-run from
Teck yuh chance, but Matty, do
Sure o' weh yuh come from so yuh got
Someweh fe come-back to!

Go a foreign, seek yuh fortune,
But noh tell nobody sey
Yuh dah-go fe seek yuh homelan
For a right deh so yuh deh!

# NOH LICKLE TWANG!
## (Not Even a Little Accent)

*This poem bemoans the fact that a recent repatriate Jamaican has returned from the United States without a trace of having been—not even a little "twang"! This, to say the least, is a highly unusual occurrence and all the more unforgivable.*

Me glad fe se's you come back bwoy,
But lawd yuh let me dung,
Me shame o' yuh soh till all o'
Me proudness drop a grung.

Yuh mean yuh goh dah 'Merica
An spen six whole mont' deh,
An come back not a piece betta
Dan how yuh did goh wey?

Bwoy yuh noh shame? Is soh you come?
Afta yuh tan soh lang!
Not even lickle language bwoy?
Not even little twang?

An yuh sista wat work ongle
One week wid 'Merican
She talk so nice now dat we have
De jooce fe undastan?

Bwoy yuh couldn' improve yuhself!
An yuh get soh much pay?
Yuh spen six mont' a foreign, an
Come back ugly same way?

Not even a drapes trouziz? or
A pass de rydim coat?
Bwoy not even a gole teet or
A gole chain roun yuh t'roat.

Suppose me las' me pass go introjooce
Yuh to a stranga
As me lamented son wat lately
Come from 'Merica!

Dem hooda laugh afta me, bwoy
Me could'n tell dem soh!
Dem hooda sey me lie, yuh was
A-spen time back a Mocho.

Noh back-ansa me bwoy, yuh talk
Too bad; shet up yuh mout,
Ah doan know how yuh an yuh puppa
Gwine to meck it out.

Ef yuh want please him meck him tink
Yuh bring back someting new.
Yuh always call him "Pa" dis evenin'
Wen him come sey "Poo".

# COLOUR-BAR

*This is a comment on the sensitivity of Jamaicans to different shades of skin-colour and the stratification of society based partly on these differences—what the sociologists call the "white bias" mentality. Indeed, the colour-fight . . . . "dung yah, Is not wid black an w'ite, but wid, Red nayga and black nayga". This is rapidly decreasing in the society at large and what was once a strong determinant of social relationships is now becoming a mere "vestigial trace" of an earlier indulgence.*

Sir Lyle eena House o' Commons
Dah-talk bout "colour-bar"
But right eena Jamaica we
Dah-have big "colour-war".

Po' Sir Lyle hooda shock fe know
Dat de colour fight dung yah
Is not wid black and w'ite, but wid
Red nayga an black nayga.

Some o' de red-kin nayga feel
Soh bex dat dem noh w'ite
Dat dem start fe cuss black nayga,
An soh dem ketch a fight.

Wen red-kin hitch too much pon w'ite
W'ite people tun dem back,
An dem fraid fe talk to black people
Less people tink dem black.

Me sorry fe po' red-kin, for
Dem don' know wey dem stan'
One granpa w'ite, an t'oder grampa
Big, black, African.

Wat a debil of a mix-up!
Wat a dickans of a plight!
Dem sey dat dem noh nayga,
Nayga sey dat dem noh w'ite.

Yuh tink de Lawd noh good to me!
Me glad me bawn nayga!
For yuh musa live in torment
Wen yuh is a malatta.

Me live eena one lickle Tung,
An me jus a-pray sey
Anancy hooda teck fas' an invite
Fire fe visit deh.

Since edication an religion
Kean stop de colour war,
We need a dose o' fire fe
Bun dung de colour bar.

## SOONER OR LATER

Sooner or later.
But mus'.
The dam going to bus' and every man will break out
and who will stop them?
The force?
What force can stop this river of man
who already know their course.
The force is a centenarian.  And that is far too old
one hundred years of brute force.  Don't tell me dem no
    cold.
"Oh"—defence force,
but dem na' defen' nott'n:
dem only come to know the ways of Babylon,
but not to partake.
Dem a fake.
Watch if dem don't defen' black man.
Stop them if you can.

The water that was used to mix the mortar for the dam
is the blood that was gathered at the slaughter of the
    lamb.
The blood of Paul Bogle, the lamb who made them need
    the force
was used to mix the mortar for the dam that stops our
    course.
The cement was his own black brethren who were the
    first policemen.
And when we reclaim water and cement we will run free
    again.
But sure.

So have-gots, have-nots,
trim-head, comb-locks, dread-knots,
is sheep from goat,
find yourself, row your own boat,
"be ready for the day"
it's been a long time coming,
but a change is on the way.
But how.
Sooner or later
but now—

right now, I and I underfed,
no clothes, no food, not even a draw to get red.
Dem want I dead?
Going dread.
Dread
But mus'.

Gloria Escoffery

## GUYANESE REFLECTIONS

### Georgetown Boy

Hear me boast, *bai,* brother:
I, clay Krishna, swimming in the trench,
blue ghosting through clouds, dropped from God's
own fingers.
Dare you catch me, now, *bai!*
Upheeled Krishna,
tip top flag-pole down in *koker* temple,
splintered.

### Rupununi Savannah

This sullen king caiman, foreign to my hill-trained eye,
loops the plain, shoals in rust, splays and joins ochre to umber
in a river of light;
makes emerald glow
in concentration camps of dust;
sand-papers trees; breeds lean cattle;
winnows horses and men, until clay beneath the skin
pools the wet harvest in mirrors for *kabouras.*
Half a year, the puddles turn clay-red eyes to winking clouds
from mountains, blue as dreams,
to a roof-edged benediction of abattoir, hangar and cactus.
Holding the built dam, the corral fence and the nurtured
         casuarina
for a dare to plumb the seed of the day's eye,
a rancher stamps out his square, beaten, bare hour of clay.
His thatched house accretes mud walls,
and a hammock swings, where a woman suckles her child.

A. L. Hendriks

## MARE NOSTRUM

Look, brother, on this archipelago
Our darling sea divides for our dismay!

Fistful of stones thrown by a fitful wrist;
Jewels on vanes of a woman's open fan;
Choose the fancy that amuses you,
You will always come down to the sea.

This sea is like a wound, unstanched,
Leaking our life away;
It is a barrier, implacable, bitter,
Blind and corrosive as racism;

Choose the fancy that amuses you,
You will always find this blue gully.

A man in his strength might walk
San Francisco to New York
Or Adelaide to Darwin,
One end of Manchuria
To the corner of Sinkiang,
But Mustique to Bequia
You need a boat or 'plane;
Swimming is for sharks, jellyfish, and tourists;

Choose the bridge you fancy,
The Caribbean drowns the dream

Met a Rastafari.
Asked him how to go,
Where to find our brethren.

232

Carriacou? Tobago?
Anguilla? Redonda? Tortola?

Africa he said, Addis Ababa,
Mek us unite with Africa
Island-man doan' understand we.

Edward Lucie-Smith

## THE HYMN TUNES

The often haunt me, these substantial ghosts,
Four-four, four-square, thumping in the brain;
Not always with the words their puritan
Plainness was made to, and yet always plain,
Bawdily forthright, loud for Lord of Hosts.
One must begin somewhere.
      Where I began

I sang off-key on Low Church, tropical
Sunday mornings; organ-swept, never doubted
That the sure tunes had reason to be sure,
That some great good would come of what I shouted.
Later, across the sea, I sang in a tall
Gothic cathedral, where all sounds endure

Long seconds in the vault, but felt no change
In what the tunes were.  And when, later still,
I learned new smut to sing to the old notes,
They stayed the same.  Nothing changed until

I woke one day to find the rules were strange
I'd thought to obey.
     Now a hymn-tune floats

Teasingly into the mind, patterns a day
To its rhythm, and nags like sudden speech
In a tongue one used to know—quietly said
Words which move forward, always out of reach;
Still, though I cannot grasp what it is they say,
God's tunes go marching through my echoing head.

Tony McNeill

## STRAIGHT SEEKING

Many believe, one day, the ship
will drop anchor, at Freeport.
But, now, it's enough to praise
high on the *spliff*. The smoke-
blackened city wounds
optimistic divines to enter
their pipes like dreams. Tonight, Jah
rears in a hundred tenements.
Missed by my maps,
still compassed by reason,
my ship sails, coolly, between
Africa and heaven.

## POSTCARD FROM JAMAICA, 22. 12. 1970
### For Bongo Jerry

Your *Mabrak* poem
is just the sort of sky-writing
eye-opener
our *Royal Reader* heads need:
Caribbean leucotomy, to *rass!*

Send the ol' nighthorse
out to grass
it did
and how
the benefits will fall
like mangoes
with no market economy
to go to
on the days to come!

*Mabrak* is a proper bitch,
ol' man
(antidote catch we, yes),
and when we read it,
we see the alternative
clean and clear
over Wareika:
touch it
and it's bound
to turn you round
on the road.

So, you' living
in you' head, now, papa?
Change not far.

## POSTCARD FROM LONDON, 23. 10. 1972

for John La Rose

When our brothers,
yours from Trinidad,
mine from Jamaica,
passed through,
the other day
from Port of Spain
and Kingston,
they looked beaten
by prosperity,
switched out
by property
and profit.

We wanted, badly,
to stop them,
in their pain,
and ask them
to look again
at themselves
and the hope of change.

But they seemed
in a hurry,
and seemed so right!
Instead,
we talked to each other.

Dennis Scott

## EPITAPH

They hanged him on a clement morning, swung
between the falling sunlight and the women's
breathing, like a black apostrophe to pain.
All morning, while the children hushed
their hop-scotch joy and the cane kept growing,
he hung there, sweet and low.

                    At least, that's how
they tell it. It was long ago.
And what can we recall of a dead slave or two,
except that, when we punctuate our island tale,
they swing like sighs across the brutal
sentences, and anger pauses
till they pass away.

# THIRD WORLD BLUES

I go among the fashionable drums
trying to keep true my own blood's subtle beat.
Something of darkness here, of jazz-horn heat,
but something too of minuet; it hums
cool in my voice, measures my heart, my feet
strictly.  And not all the blues, the concrete
jungles of this Third World, mine, can defeat
that pale and civil music when it comes.

So I make my own new way; I entreat
no tribal blessing or honor.  I build—
lonely a little—my house.  It is filled
with ghosts, with their summoning air, I greet
them all; their tunes, their joys mine.  I advance,
my feet bare to a strangely patterned dance.

# EXILE

There is a kind of loss,
like coming home
to faces; the doors open in-
differently; *they* whisper,
'Who is this, with dust
in his mouth? Who
is this new traveller?
Tell us of birds,
migrating the dull sky,
half a world round,
of Ithaca, and the tiered beast,
of that foreign city
you sent your pale card from!'

There are patterns to assure us:
at table, familiar spices;
the garden, hardly greener;
but, something has changed:
clothes we left behind;
the old affections hang loosely.
Suddenly, mouth is dumb; eyes
hurt; surprised, it is we
who have changed; glad, now,
to have practised loving
before that departure. To travel
is to return
to strangers.

Basil Smith

## TOM TOM

Give me tom-tom,
*abeng, abeng, abeng!*
Carve my features
in the likeness of
a bronze Yoruba mask!
Give me personality
the rhythm of the drum, and
make my blood boil
to the temperature of the Sahara!
Teach me to dance
the way my grandmother
has forgotten, and don't
hide
the face of Shango
from me.
Then,
and only then,
shall I be a *man.*

RETURN. . . (for Sis)


Except for the fat and raucous cancanieuse,
You'd see no one.
At first
You'd never know that he was there,
Alone
in the darkness of his memory.
Guiding as the stick that tapped out curbs for him,
It led him
far beyond
the choking bags of meal.

You only saw him
when you heard
his thumbs come
drumming
on the dumb
shop-counter board.
Then they
leading him
danced him
to the rim of memory's night
to the hum of rushing waters
to the numb—
                    ing crash of whirling forests;
                        with the black
                        Damballa
he knew his soul again. . .


Sitting there,
with Africa wrinkled over him,
        his aged veins
        Limpopo's dams,

his body seem it dead,
 done dead,
 as dead
 as de holes
 in his head.

Only the hyp-
notic beat, beat, beat-
ing of the skin on bone
on blind and silent wood,
could tell you
of the darker rush of the rushing waters,
of the deafening crash of the crashing barks,
of the joyous fear in Legba's heart. . .
 a prodigal soul
 of a wandered son
had wandered back again.


(Damballa—a god of the highway.
 Legba—The Dahomean/Haitian god of the gateway.  He is the
 crucial link between man and the other gods.)


                                        Derek Walcott



A PATRIOT TO PATRIOTS


Respect my silence. A head used to betrayals
is scared to show its tongue.

I have, too often, mistaken for an ocean
of voices the roar of city rain, seen too many

of what I thought men shrivel, finding holes
that would surprise them, like the rodent,

and the infinite variety of the rodent,
house-rat and field-rat, and church-mouse, and poets not meant

to acquire the profile of the mongoose,
the mongoose that sways to the curled flute of the serpent

mesmerised by old ideas of evil, until
in shriven panic the tainted foreteeth sink

in the neck to bite off an old question,
by which I mean, sir, what is evil? Men?

Such as the evil in history, the treachery of friends.
Listen, this is an old snake talking, be quiet,

do not cut me off. I have eaten and have seen it.
Respect my quiet. I have seen revolutions turn

into a barbarous, betrayed riot,
I mistook such voices for the mountain rain,

for a million tongues budding in flowers from asphalt,
spears and crystals of tongues,

believe in my bitterness, believe this venom.
I no longer list to such wrongs.

A cold head, used to betrayal
has shown you its tongue.

*Trinidad*
Elliott Bastien

## UPSIDE DOWN HOTEL

The tourists peel off their dollars,
their straw hat from Hawaii,
and hurry
to photograph the sun
with their body.

Middle-class grads in mohair
celebrate their success
with blonde hair.
Sapodilla girls spew out their seeds
of ebony,
and straighten their roots
with alchemy.

On the one hand, a jaguar,
on the other, caviar,
buy local officials; still there's hope
to balance the payments,
bi-focal, on a tight rope,
of monthly installments.

## RASTA FISHERMAN

Old Rasta, how that rumpled bark becomes you still
surprises me, like the moon's answer after a squall.
Once creator of silence and shade, now it's hard
put merely to survive. I know, Yacht-Owner. I

know: reluctant mariner, lost between two tides,
your moss-browed eyes hooked to a fish,
I must not raise for you
those wrecking truths your placid gaze denies.

The sun is behind you still, old man;
you ride towards your landfall.
When the time comes
beneath your barnacled feet, all earth shall be

the lion's beach, Ethiopia shining, not this
silly shifting island
of bark. I know, Yacht-Owner. I know.

Faustin Charles

## SUGAR CANE

The succulent flower bleeds molasses,
as its slender, sweet stalks bend,
beheaded in the breeze.

The green fields convulse golden sugar,
tossing the rain aside,
out-growing the sun,
and carving faces
in the sun-sliced panorama.

The reapers come at noon,
riding the cutlass-whip;
their saliva sweetens everything
in the boiling season.

Each stem is a flashing arrow,
swift in the harvest.

Cane is sweet sweat slain;
cane is labour, recognised, lost
and unrecovered;
sugar is the sweet swollen pain of the years;
sugar is slavery's immovable stain;
cane is water lying down,
and water standing up.

Cane is a slaver;
cane is bitter,
very bitter,
in the sweet blood of life.

## CALYPSONIAN

You chime sweet sounds
in rhythm and rhyme;
music pours from the arteries
of your guitar,
composed in a flood of melody;
the inspiring tune shapes hot words,
and boldly evokes
a triumphant complex of syllables.
Agile, diamond vocals stimulate
the barn dance
of your painted vernacular;
and a cynical humming-bird
joins the jump-up
of your vanguard voice,
improvising on a prosperous chorus
the Island's Angelus.

Frank John

## HUSA

I'beatin' me husa drum
all year long, an'
I ain't waitin' for no 'ficial festival;
all I want is me personal bacchanal.

*Bin-bibi-din-bong!*
*Bibi-din-bong!*

We beatin' Oil-drum,
Dus'-bin, Bamboo, Zapa-too, an'
makin' music from any ol' shoe'.

Walkin' from town to St. James,
I' moverin' like I' in Olympic Games,
and 'eatin' me roti
wit' me rum in me han',
while I' lookin' for a husa band
to join.

Brother! I' jumpin' up in the husa band
in me own mind, yes, an'
even makin' 'eadstan', an'
'oldin' plenty woman roun' them waist, an'
feelin' the people' rhythm,
as I' jumpin' up
in the husa band
in me own mind.

I ain' waitin' for no 'ficial festival;
all I want is me personal bacchanal.

*Bin-bibi-din-bong!*
*Bibi-din-bong!*

I' jumpin' up
in the husa band
in me own mind.

*Bin-bibi-din-bong!*
*Bibi-din-bong!*

## COLOUR—POEM

I make colour-poems of an easy choosing,
Trying to forget, forget, forgive.
I praise the artist, I praise the sun,
I praise black,
I praise white,
Colour-poems, easy, soothing.

    . . . . . .

Colour of cool green in a river shade,
Colour of pink saman on a black road,
Iron sugar mills etched against the sun,
Flags of bright trees flying in the exuberant wind,
In the ricefields white oxen, red machines,
Gold glare of sea-light on arcs of sand.
Cameos of brightness I collect:
Cane emerald in the ripening sun,
A small Church filled with white dresses,
By lantern-light a cartman chopping coconuts,
Red bougainvillaea on a sunlit wall,
Cloud-shadows moving on a wild hill.

    . . . . . .

Ah, brother man, I know it well!
A mild heart falsifies this art.
The greatest love is never soothing,
The greater truth is bitterness.
Pearl are the tears your mothers wept,
Black are the whips,
Grey is the ash,
Burned villages are ash,

Gold is the sweat,
Red is the blood,
Red, red are the travels of your brothers long ago.


## JAFFO, THE CALYPSONIAN


Jaffo was a great calypsonian: a fire ate up his soul to sing and
    play calypso iron music.
Even when he was small, he made many-coloured ping-pong
    drums, and searched them for the island music,
drums of beaten oil-barrel iron, daubed in triangles with stolen
    paint from a harbour warehouse.
Now, he seized the sorrow and the bawdy farce in metal-harsh
    beat and his own thick voice.
He was not famous in the tents; he went there once, and not a
    stone clapped; and he was afraid of respectable eyes;
the white-suited or gay-shirted lines of businessmen or tourists
    muffled his deep urge;
but he went back to the Indian tailor's shop and sang well, and
    to the Chinese sweet-and-sweepstake shop and sang well,
unsponsored calypsoes; and in the scrap lots near the Dry
    River, lit by one pitchoil lamp or two,
he would pound his ping-pong, and sing his hoarse voice out for
    ragged still-eyed men.
But, in the rum-shop, he was best; drinking the heavy sweet
    molasses rum, he was better than any other calypso man.
In front of the rows of dark red bottles, in the cane-scented
    rooms, his clogged throat rang and rang with staccato
    shouts.
Drunk, then, he was best; easier in pain from the cancer in his
    throat but holding the memory of it.
On the rough floors of the rum-shops, strewn with bottle-tops
    and silver-headed corks and broken green bottle-glass,

he was released from pain into remembered pain, and his thick
    voice rose and grated in brassy fear and fierce jokes.
His voice beat with bitterness and fun, as if he told of old
    things, hurt ancestral pride, and great slave humour.
He would get a rum, if he sang well; so perhaps there was that
    to it too.
He was always the best, though; he *was* the best; the ragged
    men said so, and the old men.
One month before he died, his voice thickened to a hard final
    silence.
The look of unsung calypsoes stared in his eyes, a terrible thing
    to watch in the rat-trap rum-shops.
When he could not stand for pain, he was taken to the public
    ward of the Colonial Hospital.
Rafeeq, the Indian man who in Marine Square watches the
    birds all day long for his God, was there also.
Later, he told about Jaffo in a long mad chant to the rum-shop
    men.  They laughed at the story:
until the end, Jaffo stole spoons from the harried nurses to beat
    out rhythm on his iron bedposts.

Jagdip Maraj

## FADED BEAUTY

Severed by mercenary fate,
they tried to suckle a new land.

Breasts withered
like the branches of a tree
uprooted by a savage wind, and
orphaned children, when the cane's
heat had dulled their pain,
became stiff, insensitive.

The beauty of a race faded.
Today, it breathes asthmatically
in impure forms about the country
and in venal Brahmins repeating
the Scriptures with strange intensity.

Alvin Massy

ISLANDS

1.
Morning yawns light.

Under the overturned basin of the blue
dishevelled palms bow their heads
to the wind
baring sabred fronds
which rip the celophane daylight
the new sun has begun to spread
over the morning,
still crumpled in sleep,
but thawing into an activity of birds
and animals
which resurrect from the grave of darkness
in a triumph of twitters and barks
unravelling in shrouds.

Light bares clumps of forests
scarred with handfuls of civilization
emitting smoke in puffs.
Tree trunks are standing erect
before their own shadows.

To the islands,
taut as drum skins over coral bones,
breakers with their vowels spell flagrantly
frothy bubbles with salty truths;
for water, sea water,
is the gospel of small islands,
preached by indolent rivers
veined with slender, dilating tributaries
which spew rivers into deltas,
their parables unravelling in ochre sentences
as flexible as wire.

2.
Behind bars of sunshine
our meandering beaches lie enclosed,
preserved to be mined by tourists
who sate their wanderlust
in the liquid ultramarine of cryptic eyots
sprawling on beds of sand,
torsos being kissed into tans
by the ardent lips of the sun.

To be an island is to be moored to liners
titanic and flocked with eyes,
glares shielded by dark glasses
which claw at us here
as if we were exotic primitives
unfortunate not to have known cities,
unfortunate to be black,
and assumed to be carefree as beasts,
inferior in some chromosome.


3.
We who live on islands
rooted to the algae palm of ocean
know that an island is a world
beseiged by water,
swept by gales;
an enclosure distinct and overrun
by its own bottled peculiarities.

Being intimate with islands
is to know the intoxication of fresh air,
to be rapt with the freedom of sunshine
spared from the barbarities
of continental civilization.

To be an islander
should be to consider oneself lucky,
inhabiting geographies absent even from maps.

But —


4.
History has strung these stones,
stepping across continents,
into chains of misery.

Transplanted tribes pine in squalor
which seeps its vicissitudes
into the very soul of splintered peoples,
with cryptonyms
and desecrated totems,
cast adrift without sail or oar
on an angry sea of hope,
at the mercy of high winds,

Gods dead,
lost or forgotten
in the roaring mind of some jungle
far to the south-east of time
below the equator's belt.